FARSIGHTED

ALSO BY STEVEN JOHNSON

Interface Culture:
How New Technology Transforms the Way We Create and Communicate

Emergence:
The Connected Lives of Ants, Brains, Cities, and Software

Mind Wide Open:
Your Brain and the Neuroscience of Everyday Life

Everything Bad Is Good for You:
How Today's Popular Culture Is Actually Making Us Smarter

The Ghost Map:
The Story of London's Most Terrifying Epidemic—and How It
Changed Science, Cities, and the Modern World

The Invention of Air:
A Story of Science, Faith, Revolution, and the Birth of America

Where Good Ideas Come From:
The Natural History of Innovation

Future Perfect:
The Case for Progress in a Networked Age

How We Got to Now:
Six Innovations That Made the Modern World

Wonderland:
How Play Made the Modern World

FARSIGHTED

HOW WE MAKE THE DECISIONS
THAT MATTER THE MOST

Steven Johnson

JOHN MURRAY

First published in Great Britain in 2018 by John Murray (Publishers)
An Hachette UK company

1

Copyright © Steven Johnson 2018

A CIP catalogue record for this title is available from the British Library

Hardback ISBN 978-1-473-69346-3
Trade Paperback ISBN 978-1-473-69345-6
Ebook ISBN 978-1-473-69347-0

Printed and bound by Clays Ltd, Elcograf S.p.A

John Murray policy is to use papers that are natural, renewable and
recyclable products and made from wood grown in sustainable forests.
The logging and manufacturing processes are expected to conform
to the environmental regulations of the country of origin.

John Murray (Publishers)
Carmelite House
50 Victoria Embankment
London EC4Y 0DZ

www.johnmurray.co.uk

For Dad

What theory or science is possible where the conditions and circumstances are unknown . . . and the active forces cannot be ascertained? . . . What science can there be in a matter in which, as in every practical matter, nothing can be determined and everything depends on innumerable conditions, the significance of which becomes manifest at a particular moment, and no one can tell when that moment will come?

· LEO TOLSTOY, *War and Peace*

It is now clear that the elaborate organizations that human beings have constructed in the modern world to carry out the work of production and government can only be understood as machinery for coping with the limits of man's abilities to comprehend and compute in the face of complexity and uncertainty.

· HERBERT SIMON

CONTENTS

MORAL ALGEBRA

R oughly ten thousand years ago, at the very end of the last Ice Age, a surge of glacial melt broke through a thin barrier of land that connected modern-day Brooklyn and Staten Island, creating the tidal strait now known as the Narrows—the entrance to what would subsequently become one of the world's great urban harbors, New York Bay. This geological event would prove to be both a curse and a blessing to the human beings who would subsequently live along the nearby shores. The opening to the sea was a great boon for maritime navigation, but it also allowed salt water to pour into the bay with each rising tide. Though Manhattan Island is famously bordered by two rivers, in reality, the names are misleading, since both the East River and the lower section of the Hudson are tidal estuaries, with extremely low concentrations of fresh water. The opening up of the Narrows made Manhattan Island a spectacular place to settle if you were looking for a safe harbor for your ships. But the fact that it was an island surrounded by salt water posed some real challenges if you were interested in staying hydrated, as humans are wont to do.

In the centuries before the completion of the epic aqueduct projects of the 1800s, which brought fresh drinking water to the city from rivers and reservoirs upstate, the residents of Manhattan Island—originally the Lenape tribes, then the early Dutch settlers—survived amid the salty estuaries by drinking from a small lake near the southern tip of the island, just below modern-day Canal Street. It went by several names. The Dutch called it the Kalck; later it was known as Freshwater Pond. Today it is most commonly referred to as Collect Pond. Fed by underground springs, the pond emptied out into two streams, one of which meandered toward the East River, the other draining out westward into the Hudson. At high tide, the Lenape were said to have been able to cross the entire island by canoe.

Paintings from the early eighteenth century suggest that the Collect was a tranquil and scenic spot, an oasis for early Manhattanites who wished for an afternoon's escape from the growing trade center to its south. An imposing bluff—sometimes called Bayard's Mount, sometimes Bunker Hill—loomed over the northeast edge of the pond. Climbing the hundred feet of elevation that led to its summit opened up a spectacular vista of the pond and its surrounding wetlands, with the spires and chimneys of the bustling town in the distance. "It was the grand resort in winter of our youth for skating," William Duer recalled in a memoir of early New York written in the nineteenth century, "and nothing can exceed in brilliancy and animation the prospect it presented on a fine winter day, when the icy surface was alive in skaters darting in every direction with the swiftness of the wind."

By the second half of the eighteenth century, however, commercial development had begun to spoil the Collect's bucolic setting. Tanneries set up shop on the edge of the pond, soaking the hides of animals in tannins (including poisonous chemicals from the hemlock tree) and then expelling their waste directly into the growing city's main supply of drinking water. The wetlands at the edge of the pond became a common dumping ground for dead animals—and even the occasional murder victim. In 1789, a group of concerned citizens—and a handful of real estate speculators—proposed expelling the tanneries and turning Collect Pond and the hills rising above into a public park. They hired the French architect and civil engineer Pierre Charles L'Enfant, who would design Washington, DC, several years later. An early forerunner of the public-private partnerships that would ultimately lead to the renaissance of many Manhattan parks in the late twentieth century, L'Enfant's proposal that Collect Pond Park be funded by real estate speculators buying property on the borders of the preserved public space. But the plan ultimately fell through, in large part because the project's advocates couldn't persuade the investment community that the city would ultimately expand that far north.

By 1798, the newspapers and pamphleteers were calling Collect Pond a "shocking hole" that attracted "all the leakings, scrapings, scourings, pissings, and shittings for a great distance around." With the pond's water now too polluted to drink, the city decided it was better off filling the pond and the surrounding marshlands, and building a new "luxury" neighborhood on top of it, attracting well-to-do families who wished to live outside the tumult of the city, not unlike the suburban planned communities that would sprout up on Long Island and in New Jersey a hundred and fifty years later. In 1802, the Common Council decreed that Bunker Hill be flattened and the "good and whole-some earth" from the hill be used to erase Collect Pond from the map of New York. By 1812, the freshwater springs that had slaked the thirst of Manhattan's residents for centuries had been buried belowground. No ordinary, surface-dwelling New Yorker has seen them since.

For a time in the early 1820s, a respectable neighborhood flourished over the former site of the pond. But before long, the city's attempt to erase the natural landscape of the Collect fell victim to a kind of return of the repressed. Below those fashion-able new homes, in the "good and wholesome earth" plowed in from Bunker Hill, microorganisms were steadily working their way through the organic material that had remained from Col-lect Pond's earlier life: all those decaying animal carcasses and other biomass from the wetlands.

The work of those subterranean microbes caused two prob-lems at ground level. As the biomass decomposed, the houses above began to sink into the earth. And as they sank, putrid smells began to emanate from the soil. The mildest rains would cause basements to flood with dank marsh water. Typhus out-breaks became routine in the neighborhood. Within a matter of years, the well-to-do residents had fled, and the housing stock had plummeted in value. The neighborhood soon became a mag-net for the poorest residents of the city, for African Americans escaping slavery in the South, for the new immigrants arriving from Ireland and Italy. In the squalor of its decaying infrastruc-ture, the neighborhood developed a reputation for crime and de-bauchery that echoed around the world. By the 1840s, when Charles Dickens visited it, it had become the most famous slum in the United States: Five Points.

THE FIVE-HUNDRED-YEAR MISTAKE

The story of Collect Pond is, in part, a story about a decision, or about two decisions, really. The decisions did not coincide directly in time, and neither was adjudicated by a single individual. But for the sake of shorthand we can compress them down into a simple binary: Should we preserve Collect Pond by turning it into a public park, or should we erase it? The consequences that trailed behind in the wake of that decision continue to affect the daily experiences of New Yorkers who live and work in the neighborhood today, more than two centuries later. Today, the land that was once occupied by the menacing crowds of Five Points now hosts a more wholesome, but not exactly lively, collection of government buildings and quotidian office towers. But imagine a Lower Manhattan that harbored a green oasis, perhaps the size of Boston Common, featuring a picturesque pond bordered by a rocky bluff that rivaled the heights of the man-made structures around it. We like to romanticize the Five Points era now, but the gangs of New York would have found somewhere else to assemble if the city hadn't filled the pond. The sudden drop in real estate prices that those subterranean microbes triggered certainly helped attract the immigrants who would make the city a truly cosmopolitan center, but there were other forces driving that population influx beyond the cheap housing in Five Points. City neighborhoods are still capable of great demographic and architectural change, reinventing themselves every few generations. But once you bury the pond, it never comes back.

If L'Enfant's plan had been put in place, it's entirely likely that Collect Pond Park would today stand as one of the great urban idylls in the world. The National Mall in Washington, DC, which L'Enfant also designed, attracts millions of tourists each year. Formal city parks have a longevity to them that can exceed that of castles or cemeteries or forts. The decisions to create Central and Prospect Parks continue to benefit New Yorkers a hundred and fifty years after they were first contemplated, and there is every reason to suspect that the parks will survive, more or less intact, for centuries to come. Wetlands similar to Collect Pond in the Spanish city of Seville were converted into an urban park in 1574 when the Count of Barajas drained the marsh into irrigation channels and constructed a promenade lined with poplar trees. Like many similar urban spaces, the park went through some dark times in the 1970s as a den of drugs and crime, but today it prospers, its boundaries a constant island in the sea of urban change for almost five hundred years. Only the street plan itself is more durable.

When you think about it this way, it's hard not to conceive of the decision to fill Collect Pond as a five-hundred-year mistake. But that mistake ultimately had its roots in the fact that rejecting the L'Enfant plan and burying the pond was never truly approached as a decision. It was, instead, a disorganized muddle of action and inaction. No one set out to deliberately contaminate the fresh water; the demise of the Collect was a textbook case of the tragedy of the commons. The L'Enfant plan collapsed not because the citizens didn't want to see their pond preserved, but because a handful of speculators were fantastically shortsighted about the future growth of Manhattan.

It is a truism that we suffer from chronic short-attention spans in the twenty-first century, but the fact is, we are much better at making these sorts of decisions today. A geographic element so important to the ecology of downtown Manhattan would never be destroyed without an extensive environmental impact analysis. Stakeholders would be convened to discuss alternate land-use scenarios, and participate in group decision-making rituals like design charrettes. Economists would calculate the cost to local businesses, or potential revenue from tourists visiting a landmark urban park. Participants in this conversation would be guided by a growing scientific field called decision theory—with roots in economics, behavioral psychology, and neuroscience—that has codified a number of helpful frameworks for making these kinds of long-term decisions. None of those resources were available to the residents of Manhattan at the end of the eighteenth century. We are still capable of five-hundred-year mistakes, to be sure, but we have tools and strategies now that can help us avoid them.

The ability to make deliberative, long-term decisions is one of the few truly unique characteristics of *Homo sapiens*, right alongside our technological innovation and our gift for language. And we're getting better at it. We can confront these epic choices with an intelligence and foresight that would have astonished those city planners two centuries ago.

DARWIN'S CHOICE

In July 1838, a decade or so after those fine homes began to sink into the remnants of Collect Pond, Charles Darwin sat down on the other side of the Atlantic to take notes on a decision that would, indirectly, alter the course of scientific history. Darwin was twenty-nine. He had returned from his legendary voyage around the globe on the HMS *Beagle* two years before, and was a few months away from sketching the first outline of natural selection in his notebooks, though he wouldn't publish his discovery for another two decades. The decision he was wrestling with in July would play a critical role in that agonizing delay, though it was not, strictly speaking, related to scientific questions about the origins of species. It was a different kind of decision—existential as well, but of a more personal nature: *Should I get married?*

Darwin's approach to this decision took a form that would be recognizable to many of us today: he made a list of pros and cons, dividing two facing pages in his notebook into two columns, one arguing for marriage and one against. Under the heading "Not Marry" he listed the following arguments:

> *Freedom to go where one liked*
> *Choice of Society and little of it*
> *Conversation of clever men at clubs*
> *Not forced to visit relatives and bend in every trifle*
> *Expense and anxiety of children*
> *Perhaps quarrelling*
> *Loss of Time*
> *Cannot read in the evenings*
> *Fatness and idleness*
> *Anxiety and responsibility*
> *Less money for books etc.*
> *If many children forced to gain one's bread (But then it is*
> *   very bad for one's health to work too much)*
> *Perhaps my wife won't like London; then the sentence is ban-*
> *   ishment and degradation into indolent, idle fool*

Under the heading "Marry" he compiled this list:

Children (if it Please God)

Constant companion (and friend in old age) who will feel interested in one

Object to be beloved and played with. Better than a dog anyhow

Home, & someone to take care of house

Charms of music and female chit-chat These things good for one's health—but terrible loss of time

My God, it is intolerable to think of spending one's whole life, like a neuter bee, working, working, and nothing after all—No, no, won't do

Imagine living all one's day solitary in smoky dirty London House

Only picture to yourself a nice soft wife on a sofa with good fire and books and music perhaps

Compare this vision with the dingy reality of Great Marlboro Street, London

Darwin's emotional accounting survives to this day in the Cambridge University Library archives, but we have no evidence of how he actually weighed these competing arguments against each other. We do know the decision he eventually reached, not only because he scribbled "Marry, Marry, Marry QED" at the bottom of the page, but also because he did, in fact, wed Emma Wedgwood six months after writing the words. The wedding marked the beginning of a union that would bring much happiness to Darwin, but also great intellectual conflict, as his increasingly agnostic scientific worldview clashed with Emma's religious beliefs.

Darwin's two-column technique dates back to a famous letter written a half century before by Benjamin Franklin, responding to a plea for advice from Joseph Priestley, the British chemist and political radical. Priestley was trying to decide whether to accept a job offer from the Earl of Shelburne, which would involve moving his family from Leeds to the earl's estate just east of Bath. Priestley had been friends with Franklin for several years, and so in the late summer of 1772 he wrote Franklin, who was then residing in London, and asked for his advice on this momentous career decision. Ever the master of self-improvement techniques, Franklin chose not to take sides in his reply but instead offered up a method for making the decision:

> *In the Affair of so much Importance to you, wherein you ask my Advice, I cannot for want of sufficient Premises, advise you what to determine, but if you please I will tell you how.*
>
> *When these difficult Cases occur, they are difficult chiefly because while we have them under Consideration all the Reasons pro and con are not present to the Mind at the same time; but sometimes one Set present themselves, and at other times another, the first being out of Sight. Hence the various Purposes or Inclinations that alternately prevail, and the Uncertainty that perplexes us.*
>
> *To get over this, my Way is, to divide half a Sheet of Paper by a Line into two Columns, writing over the one Pro, and over the other Con. Then during three or four Days Consideration I put down under the different Heads short Hints of the different Motives that at different Times occur to me for or against*

the Measure. When I have thus got them all together in one View, I endeavour to estimate their respective Weights; and where I find two, one on each side, that seem equal, I strike them both out: If I find a Reason pro equal to some two Reasons con, I strike out the three. If I judge some two Reasons con equal to some three Reasons pro, I strike out the five; and thus proceeding I find at length where the Ballance lies; and if after a Day or two of farther Consideration nothing new that is of Importance occurs on either side, I come to a Determination accordingly.

And tho' the Weight of Reasons cannot be taken with the Precision of Algebraic Quantities, yet when each is thus considered separately and comparatively, and the whole lies before me, I think I can judge better, and am less likely to take a rash Step; and in fact I have found great Advantage from this kind of Equation, in what may be called Moral or Prudential Algebra.

Like most pros-vs.-cons notepad sketches since, Darwin's "Marry/Not Marry" litany did not appear to utilize all the complexity of Franklin's "moral algebra." Franklin used a primitive but still powerful technique of "weighting," acknowledging that some arguments will inevitably be more meaningful than others. In Franklin's approach, the "Ballancing" stage is just as important as the initial stage of writing down entries in each column. But it seems likely that Darwin intuitively calculated the respective weights, presumably deciding that having children might in the long run matter more to him than the "conversation of clever men in clubs." In terms of simple arithmetic, there were five more entries on the "con" side of Darwin's dilemma, and yet the moral algebra in his head appears to have led to an overwhelming decision on the side of marriage.

Most of us, I suspect, have jotted down pros-vs.-cons lists at various crossroads in our personal or professional lives. (I remember my father teaching me the method on a yellow legal pad sometime in my grade-school years.) Yet Franklin's balancing act—crossing out arguments of corresponding weight—has largely been lost to history. In its simplest form, a pros-vs.-cons list is usually just a question of tallying up the arguments and determining which column is longer. But whether you integrate Franklin's more advanced techniques or not, the pros-vs.-cons list remains one of the only techniques for adjudicating a complex decision that is regularly taught. For many of us, the "science" of making hard choices has been stagnant for two centuries.

DELIBERATING

Think back to a decision you made along the lines of Darwin's or Priestley's. Perhaps it was that time you weighed leaving a comfortable but boring job for a more exciting but less predictable start-up; or the time you wrestled with undergoing a medical procedure that had a complicated mix of risk and reward. Or think of a decision you made that belonged to the public sphere: casting a vote in the Brexit referendum, say, or debating whether to hire a new principal as part of your responsibilities on a school board. Did you have a *technique* for making that decision? Or did it simply evolve as a series of informal conversations and background mulling? I suspect most of us would say the latter; at best, our techniques would not be all that different from Darwin's jotting down notes in two columns on a piece of paper and tallying up the results.

The craft of making farsighted choices—decisions that require long periods of deliberation, decisions whose consequences might last for years, if not centuries, as in the case of Collect Pond—is a strangely underappreciated skill. Think about the long list of skills we teach high school students: how to factor quadratic equations; how to diagram the cell cycle; how to write a good topic sentence. Or we teach skills with a more vocational goal: computer programming, or some kind of mechanical expertise. Yet you will almost never see a course devoted to the art and science of decision-making, despite the fact that the ability to make informed and creative decisions is a skill that applies to every aspect of our lives: our work environments; our domestic roles as parents or family members; our civic lives as voters, activists, or elected officials; and our economic existence managing our monthly budget or planning for retirement.

Ironically, in recent years, we have seen a surge in popular books about decision-making, but most of them have focused on a very different kind of decision: the flash judgments and gut impressions profiled in books like *Blink* and *How We Decide*, many of them building on the pioneering research into the emotional brain associated with scientists like Antonio Damasio and Joseph LeDoux. Daniel Kahneman's brilliant *Thinking, Fast and Slow* introduced the notion of the brain as divided between two distinct systems, both of which are implicated in the decision-making process. System 1 is the intuitive, fast-acting, emotionally charged part of the brain; System 2 is what we call on when we have to consciously think through a situation. These are undeniably powerful categories in thinking about thinking, but Kahneman's work—much of it a collaboration with the late Amos Tversky—has largely focused on the idiosyncrasies and irrationalities of System 1. This new model of the brain is helpful in understanding all sorts of dysfunctions, small and large, that plague us in the modern world. We have learned how our brains can be manipulated by credit card schemes and predatory mortgage lenders; we've learned why we choose certain brands over others, and why we sometimes fall prey to misleading first impressions in deciding whether to trust someone we've just met. But if you read through the clinical research, most of the experiments behind the science tend to sound something like this:

> **Problem 1:** *Which do you choose? Get $900 for sure OR 90 percent chance to get $1,000*

> **Problem 2:** *Which do you choose? Lose $900 for sure OR 90 percent chance to lose $1,000*

> **Problem 3:** *In addition to whatever you own, you have been given $1,000. You are now asked to choose one of these options: 50 percent chance to win $1,000 OR get $500 for sure*

> **Problem 4:** *In addition to whatever you own, you have been given $2,000. You are now asked to choose one of these options: 50 percent chance to lose $1,000 OR lose $500 for sure*

You could fill an entire book with examples of this kind of experiment, and the results that these studies have generated have indeed been eye-opening and sometimes counterintuitive. But as you read through the studies, you start to notice a recurring absence: none of the choices being presented to the experimental subjects look anything like the decision to bury Collect Pond or Priestley's choice to take on a new patron. Instead, the decisions almost invariably take the form of little puzzles, closer to the choices you make at a blackjack table than the kind of choice that Darwin was contemplating in his notebook. Fields like behavioral economics have been built on the foundation of these abstract experiments, where scientists ask their subjects to wager on a few arbitrary outcomes, each with different probabilities attached to them. There's a reason why so many of the questions take this form: these are precisely the kinds of decisions that can be tested in a lab.

But when we look back at the trajectory of our lives, and of history itself, I think most of us would agree that the decisions that ultimately matter the most do not—or at least should not—rely heavily on instincts and intuition to do their calculations. They're decisions that require slow thinking, not fast. While they are no doubt influenced by the emotional shortcuts of our gut reactions, they rely on deliberative thought, not instant responses. We take time in making them, precisely because they involve complex problems with multiple variables. Those properties necessarily make the logical and emotional networks behind these decisions more opaque to the researchers, given the obvious ethical and practical limitations that make it challenging for scientists to study choices of this magnitude. Asking someone to choose one candy bar over another is easy enough to do in the lab; asking someone to decide whether or not to marry is quite a bit more difficult to engineer.

But that does not mean the tools available to us in making hard choices have not improved mightily since Priestley's day. Most of the important research in this multidisciplinary field has been conducted on small- to medium-sized group decisions: a team of business colleagues debating whether to launch a new product; a group of military advisors weighing different options for an invasion; a community board trying to decide on the proper guidelines for development in a gentrifying neighborhood; a jury determining the guilt or innocence of a fellow citizen. For good reason, these sorts of decisions are formally described as "deliberative" decisions. When we first encounter the accused burglar on a jury trial, we may well have an instinctive response of guilt or innocence that comes to us through a quick assessment of his or her demeanor or facial expression, or through our own preexisting attitudes toward crime and law enforcement. But systems engineered to promote deliberative decision-making are specifically designed to keep us from naively falling into those preconceived assumptions, precisely because they are not likely to steer us toward the correct decision. We need time to deliberate, to weigh the options, to listen to different points of view before we render a judgment.

We don't need to rely exclusively on social psychology experiments to cultivate our decision-making skills. Recent history abounds with case studies where complex decisions were made by groups of people who consciously adopted strategies and routines designed to produce more farsighted results. We have a lot to learn from studying those decisions, both because we can apply those techniques to our own choices and because we can use that knowledge to evaluate the decision-making skills of our leaders and colleagues and peers. You almost never hear a political debate—or a shareholder meeting—where one of the candidates or executives is asked how he or she goes about making a decision, but in the end, there may be no more valuable skill for someone in any kind of leadership position. Courage, charisma, intelligence—all the usual attributes we judge when we consider voting for someone pale in comparison to the one fundamental question: Will he or she make good choices when confronted with a complex situation? Intelligence or confidence or intuition can only take us so far when we reach one of those difficult crossroads. In a sense, individual attributes are not sufficient. What a "decider"—to use George W. Bush's much-mocked term—needs in those circumstances is not a *talent* for decision-making. Instead, what he or she needs is a *routine* or a *practice*—a specific set of steps for confronting the problem, exploring its unique properties, weighing the options.

It turns out that there is great drama and intensity in watching a group of minds wrestling with a complex decision. (Some of the most powerful passages in literature capture this experience, as we will see.) But that slower, more contemplative narrative is often overshadowed by more abrupt events: a fiery speech, a military invasion, a dramatic product launch. We tend to fast-forward to the outcomes of complex decisions, skipping over the journey that led to them. But sometimes, when it matters most, we need to rewind the tape.

THE COMPOUND

In August 2010, the Pakistani courier Ibrahim Saeed Ahmed—also known as "al-Kuwaiti," among other aliases—drove two hours east from the arid valley city of Peshawar up into the Sarban Hills where the city of Abbottabad is located. With known ties to Osama bin Laden and a number of other high-level al-Qaeda operatives, al-Kuwaiti had been a person of interest for the CIA for several years. A Pakistani asset gathering intelligence for the CIA had identified al-Kuwaiti's white Suzuki jeep in Peshawar and followed him without discovery all the way to a suburb at the outskirts of Abbottabad, a journey that ended on a dirt road leading to a ramshackle compound surrounded by fifteen-foot-high concrete walls topped with barbed wire. After al-Kuwaiti entered the compound, the Pakistani operative sent word back to the CIA that his target had been welcomed into a building that appeared to possess more elaborate security than other houses in the neighborhood. Something seemed suspicious about the setting.

That deft act of surveillance set in motion a chain of events that would eventually lead to the legendary May 2011 raid and the death of Osama bin Laden, who had managed to live in the compound in relative comfort—certainly compared to the cave-dwelling that many suspected he had resorted to—for almost five years. The story of the attack on bin Laden's unlikely residence—with Black Hawk helicopters descending on the compound in the early morning hours—has been widely covered as a brilliantly executed military operation, and a resilient one, in that it survived what could easily have been a catastrophic failure when one of the helicopters crashed while attempting to hover over the compound's interior. The actions taken that night tell a story about bravery, near-flawless teamwork, and quick thinking under almost unimaginable pressure. Not surprisingly, it has been the subject of blockbuster Hollywood films and high-profile TV documentaries, as well as a number of bestselling books.

But the wider story behind the raid—not just the actions taken that night, but the nine months of debate and deliberation that resulted in the Abbottabad attack—helps explain why the talent for making hard choices has been generally neglected in our schools and the wider culture. We have a tendency to emphasize the *results* of good decisions and not the process that led to the decision itself. The Abbottabad raid was a triumph of military institutions like the Navy SEALs and the satellite technology that enabled them to analyze the compound with enough precision to plan the attack. But beneath all that spectacular force and daring, a slower and less headline-worthy process had made the raid possible in the first place, a process that explicitly drew on our new understanding about how to make hard choices. The technology deployed to track down bin Laden was state-of-the-art, from the satellites to the Black Hawks. But so was the decision-making. The irony is, most of us ordinary civilians have almost nothing to learn from the story of the raid itself. But we have everything to learn from the decision process that set it in motion. The vast majority of us will never have to land a helicopter in a small courtyard under the cover of darkness. But all of us will confront challenging decisions in our lives, the outcomes of which can be improved by learning from the internal deliberations that led to the killing of bin Laden.

When news first reached the CIA's headquarters at Langley that their operative had tracked al-Kuwaiti to a mysterious compound on the outskirts of Abbottabad, almost no one in the CIA suspected they had stumbled across Osama bin Laden's actual hideout. The consensus was that bin Laden was living in some remote region, not unlike the caves outside Tora Bora where US forces had nearly captured him eight years before. The compound itself was situated less than a mile from the Pakistan Military Academy; many of bin Laden's neighbors were members of the Pakistan military. Pakistan was supposed to be our ally in the war on terror. The idea that the man who had engineered the 9/11 plot might be living in the middle of a Pakistan military community seemed preposterous.

But early reconnaissance on the compound only heightened the mystery. The CIA quickly determined that the compound had no phone lines or Internet, and the residents burned their own trash.

Al-Kuwaiti's presence suggested that the building had some connection to al-Qaeda, but the construction costs alone—estimated at more than $200,000—were puzzling: Why would the cash-starved terror network spend so much money on a building in suburban Abbottabad? According to Peter Bergen's account of the hunt for bin Laden, CIA chief Leon Panetta was briefed about al-Kuwaiti's visit in August 2010. Officials described the compound—somewhat aggressively—as a "fortress." The word caught Panetta's attention, and he ordered the officials to pursue "every possible operation avenue" to discover who was living behind those concrete walls.

The decision process that led to the killing of Osama bin Laden was, ultimately, a sequence of two very different kinds of decisions. The first took the form of a mystery: the CIA had to decide who was living inside the enigmatic compound. The second decision arose once they had reached reasonable certainty that the structure housed al-Qaeda's leader: how to get into the compound and either capture or kill bin Laden, assuming the first decision had been correct. The first decision was epistemological: How can we *know* for certain the identity of the people living in this building on the other side of the planet? Making the decision involved a kind of detective work: piecing together clues from a wide range of sources. The second decision revolved around actions and their consequences: If we simply flatten the compound with a B-2 bombing run, will we ever know for sure that bin Laden was on the premises? If we send in a special ops team to extract him, what happens if they run into trouble on the ground? And even if they're successful, should they attempt to capture bin Laden alive?

As it happened, each of these decisions was shadowed by a similar decision in the past that had gone horribly wrong. The Bush administration had wrestled with a comparable epistemological decision—does Saddam Hussein possess weapons of mass destruction?—with disastrous consequences eight years before. And the decision to launch the raid on the compound had echoes both of Jimmy Carter's failed helicopter rescue of the Iranian hostages and John F. Kennedy's botched Bay of Pigs invasion. These decisions had been made by smart people working in good faith to make the correct call. The decisions were deliberated on for months, and yet they ended in catastrophic failure. In a sense you can see the ultimate triumph of the bin Laden raid as a rare example of an institution learning from its mistakes by deliberately improving the *process* that had led to those past mistakes.

Many hard choices turn out to contain interior decisions that have to be adjudicated separately, and often in some kind of preordained sequence, as in the Abbottabad raid. To make the right choice, you have to figure out how to structure the decision properly, which is itself an important skill. With the pursuit of bin Laden, the CIA had to make a decision about who was in the compound, and then it had to make a decision about how to attack the compound. But each of those decisions was itself made up of two distinct phases, sometimes called divergence and consensus phases. In a divergence phase, the key objective is to get as many perspectives and variables on the table as possible through exploratory exercises designed to reveal new possibilities. Sometimes those possibilities take the form of information that might influence your ultimate choice of which path to take; sometimes those possibilities take the form of entirely new paths that you didn't contemplate at the beginning of the process. In the consensus phase, the open-ended exploration of new possibilities reverses course, and the group begins to narrow down its options, seeking agreement on the correct path. Each phase requires a distinct set of cognitive tools and collaborative models to succeed. Of course, most of us don't separate the two phases in our minds at all. We just look at the options, have a few informal meetings, and make a decision, either through some kind of show of hands or an individual assessment.

In the bin Laden pursuit, the CIA deliberately set up a divergence phase at both stages of its investigation into that mysterious compound. A few weeks after Panetta first heard word of the "fortress" on the edge of Abbottabad, his chief of staff ordered the bin Laden team to conjure up twenty-five different ways of identifying the occupants of the compound. They were explicitly told that no idea was too crazy. This was the exploratory phase, after all. The goal was to generate more possibilities, not narrow the field. The analysts turned out to be all too willing to propose unlikely schemes. "One idea was to throw in foul-smelling stink bombs to flush out the occupants of the compound," Bergen writes. "Another was to play on the presumed religious fanaticism of the compound's inhabitants and broadcast from loudspeakers outside the compound what purported to be the 'Voice of Allah,' saying, 'You are commanded to come out into the street!'" In the end, they proposed *thirty-seven* ways of getting surreptitious access to the compound. Most of them turned out to be utterly useless in identifying the occupants, dead ends in the exploratory phase. But some of the schemes ended up opening new paths. One of those paths would eventually lead to the death of Osama bin Laden.

BOUNDED RATIONALITY

What is it about complex decisions that makes them so challenging? For most of the preceding two centuries, our understanding of decision-making largely revolved around the concept of "rational choice" from classical economics. When people confronted a decision point in their lives—whether it involved buying a car or moving to California or voting to leave the European Union—they evaluated the options available to them and considered the relative benefits and costs of each potential outcome (in economics-speak, the "marginal utility" of each option). And then they simply picked the winner: the path that would lead to the most useful destination, the one that satisfied their needs or produced the most happiness with minimal cost.

If you had to specify a point in our intellectual history where that classical foundation first began to crumble, you might well land on the speech Herbert Simon delivered in Stockholm in 1958 when accepting the Nobel Prize in Economic Sciences. Simon's work had explored all the ways in which the "rational choice" framework concealed the much murkier reality of choices made in the real world. For rational choice to make sense, it required four significant leaps of faith:

> *The classical model calls for knowledge of all the alternatives that are open to choice. It calls for complete knowledge of, or ability to compute, the consequences that will follow on each of the alternatives. It calls for certainty in the decision-maker's present and future evaluation of these consequences. It calls for the ability to compare consequences, no matter how diverse and heterogeneous, in terms of some consistent measure of utility.*

Think of a decision like the one to bury Collect Pond in these classical terms. Were all the potential options visible to the decision-makers? Were the decision-makers fully aware of the consequences of each potential path? Of course not. You might be able to narrow a decision down to a fixed set of alternatives with reasonably predictable consequences if you were deciding whether to buy frozen pizza or filet mignon for dinner tonight. But in a situation as complex as the one facing the residents of Manhattan circa 1800, the rational choice is not so easily computed. Simon proposed supplementing the elegant (but reductive) formula of rational choice with the notion of what he called "bounded rationality": decision-makers cannot simply wish away the uncertainty and open-endedness of the choices they confront. They have to develop strategies that specifically address those challenges.

In the sixty years that have passed since Simon's address, researchers in many fields have expanded our understanding of bounded rationality. We now understand that farsighted decisions are challenging for many different reasons. They involve multiple interacting variables; they demand thinking that covers a full spectrum of different experiences and scales; they force us to predict the future with varying levels of certainty. They often feature conflicting objectives, or potential useful options that are not visible at first glance. And they are vulnerable to the distortions introduced by individual "System 1" thinking, and by the failings of groupthink. There are eight primary factors that contribute to the challenge of farsighted decision-making.

Complex decisions involve multiple variables. When we mull one of those classic lab experiment decisions—"Get $900 for sure OR 90% chance to get $1,000"—there are indeed subtle ways in which our brains steer us to irrational choices, but there are no hidden factors in the choice, no layers that need to be un-

covered. Even the unpredictable element—the 90 percent chance—
is clearly defined. But in a hard choice—what to do with Collect
Pond, how to determine if bin Laden is living in Abbottabad—
there can be hundreds of potential variables that might impact
the decision and its ultimate consequences. Even intimate decisions can involve a significant number of factors: Darwin's
pros-vs.-cons list calculated the impact of marriage on his social
life with "men in clubs," his desire to have children, his financial stability, his need for romantic companionship, his intellectual ambitions, and more. And in many complex decisions, key
variables are not evident at the outset; they have to be uncovered.

Complex decisions require full-spectrum analysis. Imagine the
many scales of human experience as slices of the frequency spectrum of audible sound. When we adjust the EQ of a recording, we
are zooming in on one of those slices: we want to turn the low
end down a bit so the bass doesn't rumble, or boost the midrange
so we can hear the vocals. Music producers have surgically precise
tools that allow them to target astonishingly narrow slices of that
spectrum, tools that let you extract the background hum of a
120 Hz electric current from a mix, but nothing else. With sound,
there are two polar extremes of listening: narrowband and full
spectrum. You can carve everything else out of the mix and only
hear that hum, or you can listen to the whole orchestra.

Decisions can be imagined in a similar way. The blizzard of
decisions that you make over the course of an ordinary day are
largely narrowband in nature, like choosing this brand of ketchup
over that one or deciding which route to take on your morning
commute. But the decisions that really matter in life, the hard
choices, can't be understood on a single scale. It's not just that
they contain multiple variables; it's also that those variables draw

on completely different frames of reference. They are multidisciplinary. Consider the public decisions of voting or rendering a jury verdict. To make those decisions well, you need to force your mind out of its narrowband priorities. You have to think about a problem from multiple perspectives. Voting for a candidate demands that you think about the temperament of the politicians in the race, their economic positions and their impact on your own pocketbook, the global forces likely to shape their tenure in elected office, their ability to work with their colleagues in government, and many other variables. A juror has to cognitively shift from the microscopic realm of forensic evidence to the arcane history of legal precedent to the intuitive psychology of reading the facial expressions of witnesses on the stand. Most of us have a powerful urge to retreat to narrowband assessments: *She just looks guilty; I'm voting for the guy who will lower my taxes.* But we decide better when we break out of the myopia of the single scale.

Complex decisions force us to predict the future. Most decisions, big or small, are fundamentally predictions about the future. I choose vanilla ice cream over chocolate because I can predict, with an accuracy long-buffered by experience, that I will enjoy the vanilla more than the chocolate. The consequences of the US government staging a raid on a private residence in Pakistan were not quite as easy to predict. A modern-day environmental planner might well include microorganisms in weighing the decision to bury Collect Pond, since cleaning up the drinking water involves ridding it of dangerous bacteria. But it seems unlikely that she would have included the microorganisms that caused the fill beneath Five Points to degrade, thus triggering the collapse of housing values in the neighborhood. These are the very definition of chaotic systems: they contain hundreds, if not thousands, of independent variables, all locked into feedback-heavy relation-ships, where small agents can trigger unimagined tidal waves.

Complex decisions involve varied levels of uncertainty. In many of the classic lab experiments of behavioral economics, psycholo-gists may introduce a level of uncertainty to the decision being studied, but that uncertainty itself is clearly defined by the terms of the experiment: If you choose the 90 percent route versus the sure thing, you know exactly how much uncertainty you are will-ing to tolerate. But complex decisions in the real world necessar-ily involve different levels of uncertainty: If you are contemplating a move from New York to California, you can be certain that the winter temperatures will be, on average, warmer if you move, but the question of whether your children will thrive in the state's public schools is necessarily more ambiguous. Yet in many cases, the outcomes with the highest uncertainty are the ones we care about the most.

Complex decisions often involve conflicting objectives. Narrow-band decisions are easy because you don't have the intermingling of signals from different parts of the spectrum. You don't have to think about microorganisms altering property values, or how your professional ambition as a scientist might affect your desire for emotional intimacy with a spouse. The chains of causality are simpler. But full spectrum also poses challenges because people often have incompatible value systems at different points on the spectrum. It's easy to go with your heart when you are only cal-culating the impact on your emotional state. It's much harder when your heart conflicts with your politics, or your community roots, or your financial needs—or all three. And, of course, these conflicts become even more severe when the decision involves multiple stakeholders or an entire community.

Complex decisions harbor undiscovered options. As Simon observed, hard choices also confound us because the choices available to us are often not fully defined. They may appear, at first glance, to offer a binary set of options: choose A or choose B. But often the best decision—the decision that somehow finds the most artful balance between the competing bands of the spectrum—turns out to be an option that wasn't visible at the outset.

Complex decisions are prone to System 1 failings. For the individual contemplating a complex decision, the quirks of System 1 thinking can distort the way the choice is framed or the potential virtues of the choices on the table. Loss aversion, confirmation bias, the availability heuristic—all the shortcuts that make it easy to get through the simple problems of life can turn out to be liabilities when we face a true crossroads.

Complex decisions are vulnerable to failures of collective intelligence. Groups by definition bringing a wider set of perspective and knowledge to the table. Large, diverse groups can be vital to the divergent stage of a decision, introducing new possibilities, exposing unseen risks. But groups are vulnerable to many failings of their own, including collective biases or distortions that arise from the social dynamics of human interaction. The word "groupthink" is a pejorative for a reason. As we will see, many of the techniques that have been developed to augment complex decision-making have been specifically engineered to steer around the potential blind spots or biases of group behavior, and to uncover the wide range of knowledge that a well-curated group possesses.

These eight factors are the shoals on which countless long-term decisions have foundered. It is almost impossible to avoid them all in navigating a difficult choice. But over the decades that have passed since Simon first proposed his notion of bounded rationality, decision-makers in many fields have developed a set of practices that help us steer around some of them, or at least fortify our vessel so that the inevitable collisions do less damage as we make our way to safe harbor.

FINGERPRINTS AND THREADLIKE PRESSURES

In the simplest terms, deliberative decisions involve three steps, designed specifically to overcome the unique challenges of a hard choice: we build an accurate, full-spectrum *map* of all the variables, and the potential paths available to us; we make *predictions* about where all those different paths might lead us, given the variables at play; we reach a *decision* on a path by weighing the various outcomes against our overarching objectives. The first three chapters explore the techniques for making those group decisions, roughly following the sequence that most decision paths unfold along: mapping, predicting, and ultimately making the choice. The final two chapters take a more speculative look at decisions made on the two extremes: mass decisions about broader issues, like the decision we face in battling climate change; and personal decisions, like the one Darwin wrestled with in his notebook.

There's a wonderful scene in the first half of George Eliot's *Middlemarch* that captures the challenges of complex decision-making. (We'll come back to *Middlemarch* and an even more famous decision from the book in the final chapter.) The scene follows the internal monologue of an ambitious young physician named Tertius Lydgate in 1830s England as he weighs a particularly vexing group decision: whether to replace the amiable local vicar, Camden Farebrother, with a new chaplain named Tyke, who is supported by Nicholas Bulstrode, the sanctimonious town banker and the main source of funding for Lydgate's hospital. Lydgate has struck up a friendship with Farebrother, though he disapproves of the vicar's gambling habit. As a town council meeting approaches, Lydgate churns through his options:

> He did not like frustrating his own best purposes by getting on bad terms with Bulstrode; he did not like voting against Farebrother, and helping to deprive him of function and salary; and the question occurred whether the additional forty pounds might not leave the Vicar free from that ignoble care about winning at cards. Moreover, Lydgate did not like the consciousness that in voting for Tyke he should be voting on the side obviously convenient for himself. But would the end really be his own convenience? Other people would say so, and would allege that he was currying favor with Bulstrode for the sake of making himself important and getting on in the world. What then? He for his own part knew that if his personal prospects simply had been concerned, he would not have cared a rotten nut for the banker's friendship or enmity. What he really cared for was a medium for his work, a vehicle for his ideas; and after all, was he not bound to prefer the object of getting a good hospital, where he could demonstrate the specific distinctions of fever and test therapeutic results, before anything else connected with this chaplaincy? For the first time Lydgate was feeling the hampering threadlike pressure of small social conditions, and their frustrating complexity.

What is striking here is, first, the nuance of the portrait of the deciding mind: all those "threadlike pressures" drawn in exacting detail. (Indeed, the excerpt above is only a fraction of Eliot's treatment of Lydgate's musings on this one choice, which take up the good part of a chapter.) But the pressures themselves originate with forces wider and more varied than the individual mind. In just this one paragraph, Lydgate is wrestling with his personal friendship with Farebrother; his moral objections to Farebrother's weakness for cards; the social stigma of being seen as voting on the side of his patron; the economic cost of potentially betraying his patron in a public forum; the threat to his intellectual ambitions if Bulstrode should turn on him; and the opportunities for enhancing the health of the Middlemarch community, thanks to his growing scientific understanding of the "specific distinctions of fever." The choice itself is binary: Farebrother or Tyke. But the array of factors that shape the choice are scattered across multiple scales, from the intimacy of personal connection to long-term trends in medical science. And the choice is further confounded by the fact that Lydgate himself has conflicting objectives: He wants to see his hospital funded, but he doesn't want to be mocked by the community for "currying favor" with the banker.

You can see in Lydgate's tortured internal monologue a mind wrestling with both the mapping and predictive phase of a hard choice: thinking through all the layers of the decision, and speculating on what will happen if he makes one choice versus another. In Lydgate's mind—as in Darwin's pros-vs.-cons list—the two phases meld together into one. But it turns out we are much better off when we consider those two kinds of problems separately: mapping the decision and all of its "threadlike pressures" and then predicting the future outcomes that those pressures are likely to create.

Skeptics might argue, not without reason, that there is

something about complex decisions that fundamentally resists one-size-fits-all prescriptions. There are simply too many variables, interacting in nonlinear ways, to wrestle them down into predictable patterns. The complexity of the problem makes it singular. Every long-term decision is a snowflake, or a fingerprint: unique, never to be repeated, so different from its peers that we can't shovel it into formulaic categories. This is the position that Tolstoy's Prince Andrei adopts in a memorable passage from *War and Peace*, challenging the "science of warfare" that the Russian generals believe they have mastered. Anticipating Herbert Simon's Nobel speech, Prince Andrei asks: "What theory or science is possible where the conditions and circumstances are unknown, and the active forces cannot be ascertained?"

Tolstoy intended the question to be a rhetorical one, but you can think of this book as an attempt to give it a proper answer. Part of the answer is that science has endowed us with tools to better perceive the nuances of complex situations, tools that didn't exist in Tolstoy's or Darwin's time. The fact that each fingerprint is unique hasn't stopped scientists from understanding how fingerprints form in the first place, or even why they form such unpredictable shapes. But the most important progress in the science of fingerprints has come from exponential advances in our ability to tell them all apart, discerning the unique whorls that differentiate one person's print from another's. Science does not always compress the teeming complexity of the world into compact formulas, the way Tolstoy's military planners tried to compress the chaos of the battlefield into the "science of warfare." Sometimes science expands. Sometimes it helps us apprehend the particulars of life, all the details that might escape a less observant eye. When this book draws upon scientific research into decision-making, it is largely drawing from that expansive mode, from studies that help us see past our biases and stereotypes and first impressions.

But another part of the answer to Prince Andrei's question is to admit that he has a point: there are limits to what the scientific lens can reveal about the full range of human experiences, whether those experiences unfold on the battlefield or in a small town-council meeting debating who to choose as the next vicar. In those environments, as Tolstoy put it, "everything depends on innumerable conditions, the significance of which becomes manifest at a particular moment, and no one can tell when that moment will come." An individual human life is a unique cocktail of chance and circumstance, made all the more complex when it is muddled, as it invariably is, by other spirits. Something gets lost when you reduce all that to chemistry.

But as the behavioral economists like to remind us, we are already prone to all sorts of reductions as a species. It's not just the scientists. We compress complex reality down into abbreviated heuristics that often work beautifully in everyday life for high-frequency, low-significance decisions. Because we are an unusually clever and self-reflective species, we long ago realized that we needed help overcoming those reductive instincts when it really matters. And so we invented a tool called storytelling. At first, some of our stories were even more reductive than the sciences would prove to be: allegories and parables and morality plays that compressed the flux of real life down to archetypal moral messages. But over time the stories grew more adept at describing the true complexity of lived experience, the whorls and the threadlike pressures. One of the crowning achievements of that growth is the realist novel. That, of course, is the latent implication of Prince Andrei's question: "innumerable conditions made meaningful only in unpredictable moments" would fare well as a description of both *War and Peace* and *Middlemarch*, arguably the two totemic works in the realist canon. What gives the novel the grain of truth lies precisely in the way it doesn't quite run along the expected grooves, the way it dramatizes all the forces and unpredictable variables that shape the choices humans confront at the most meaningful moments of their lives.

When we read those novels—or similarly rich biographies of historical figures—we are not just entertaining ourselves; we are also rehearsing for our own real-world experiences. More than anything else, when we find ourselves confronting one of life's hard choices, we need to see it on its own terms, with fresh eyes. For that we have art as much as science. We have stories—realist novels, yes, but also, as we will see, other genres of stories that have been deliberately crafted to help us perceive a larger slice of the spectrum and prepare us for uncertain outcomes. They have names like scenario plans, war games, ensemble simulations, premortems. None of them should be mistaken for great art. But what they share with the realist novel is an almost miraculous ability to get us to see the world more sharply, to see each whorl in the fingerprint as it really is. They don't give us simple prescriptions. But they do give us something almost as valuable: *practice*.

There is wisdom in understanding a decision because it resembles some past crossroads, either drawn from your personal experience or the anecdotes of friends or colleagues or the clinical studies of scientists. But there is wisdom, too, in seeing all the ways the decision breaks from the past, in appreciating its singular properties. It is the hypothesis of this book that this way of seeing can be taught.

MAPPING

> If we had a keen vision and feeling of all ordinary
> human life, it would be like hearing the grass grow and
> the squirrel's heart beat, and we should die of that roar
> which lies on the other side of silence. As it is, the
> quickest of us walk about well wadded with stupidity.
>
> · GEORGE ELIOT, *MIDDLEMARCH*

Long before Brooklyn became one of the most densely populated urban regions in the country, back when it was a modest hamlet on a bluff overlooking the prosperous harbor town of New York, a long ridge of thick woods ran through the center of the borough's current borders, stretching from present-day Greenwood Cemetery through Prospect Park all the way to Cypress Hill. Locals had given it a name straight out of Tolkien: the Heights of Gowan.

As geological formations go, the Heights of Gowan were hardly unusual. At their peak, they rose only two hundred feet over the glacier-flattened plains and tidal ponds of Long Island. Yet in the summer of 1776, the Heights found themselves at the center of world history. Just months before, the British had endured a humiliating retreat from Boston. Capturing New York, the trading center of the colonies and the gateway to the mighty Hudson (then called the North River), was the obvious counter-move, given the British dominance in sea power.

Perched at the tip of an island facing a vast bay, New York presented an easy target for the king's armada. The problem lay in holding on to the city. From the fortified bluffs of modern-day Brooklyn Heights on Long Island, downtown New York could be continuously bombarded. "For should the enemy take hold New York while we hold on to Long Island, they will find it almost impossible to subsist," American general Charles Lee wrote. To hold on to the city without heavy casualties, British commander William Howe would ultimately need to capture Brooklyn. And Brooklyn was protected by the Heights of Gowan. It was not the topography that created the natural barricade but rather the dense canopy of eastern deciduous forest that covered the ridge, with its towering oaks and hickory trees and heavy thicket on the ground. An army could not hope to move a large mass of men and equipment through such an environment, and besides, if the battle turned into the forest, the Revolutionary forces would have the upper hand.

The Heights were not a perfect barricade, however. Four roads cut through the woods from south to north: Gowanus, Flatbush, Bedford, and a small gorge that went by the name Jamaica Pass. If the British chose not to make a direct assault on Brooklyn or Manhattan from the water, they would likely have to move their troops through these narrow conduits.

From the moment word spread in early June that the British ships had left Halifax, headed south, it was clear to everyone that the British would attempt to take New York. The question was how they would go about doing it. That was the crux of the decision that confronted George Washington in the long, quiet summer of 1776, as an imposing armada—the "four hundred ships in New York Harbor" that appear in the opening minutes of *Hamilton*—took anchor off the shores of Staten Island. Should he defend Manhattan or Brooklyn? Or, perhaps, should he concede that New York was beyond defending, a hopeless cause, and move the fight to more promising ground?

Washington was confronting a classic example of a full-spectrum decision, one that required him to think simultaneously on several different scales of experience. To make the right decision, Washington had to think about the topography of the land, those ridges and bluffs and beaches; he had to think about the notoriously unpredictable currents of the East River, which could wreak havoc on any attempt to rapidly move troops between New York and Brooklyn; he had to think about the physics of war—the cannons of those British warships, and the durability of the defenses he had built along the waterfront of the city; he had to think of the morale of his troops, and the Continental Congress back in Philadelphia, sending him directives demanding that he not surrender such a valuable city and harbor. The decision had an ethical dimension as well: Faced with such an imposing enemy, was it right for Washington to send so many young lives into a battle they were likely to lose?

Washington had no shortage of variables to consider, but he also had something else: time. From the moment the British abandoned Boston, Washington had been wrestling with the question of New York's defense. He had arrived and established residence at 1 Broadway, at the very tip of the island, in early April. With the counsel of General Lee and the brilliant general Nathanael Greene, he had been surveying and directing the fortification of New York and Brooklyn for months before the British armada appeared. By the time General Howe had finally ordered his men to make their assault on New York in late August, Washington had had nearly half a year to decide on the best strategy for defending the city.

When Washington finally did make his decision, it would prove to be the most catastrophic of his entire career.

THE BLIND SPOT

Part of what the epic choices of literature and history have to teach us lies in the inverted wisdom of failed decisions, the mistakes we can learn from, either because they point to some nagging feature of the human mind that undermines us or some failing of our environment that sends our choices down the wrong path.

In the summer of 1776, Washington's initial mistake was to even defend New York in the first place. It was, by every account, a hopeless cause. Outnumbered by the British two to one, and facing an impossible disadvantage in terms of sea power, the smart move would have been to surrender the city. "It is so encircled by deep, navigable water that whoever commands the sea must command the town," Lee wrote to Washington. But Washington seemed incapable of contemplating giving up such a valuable asset so early in the fight.

After he had committed to defending the city, Washington made a series of crucial tactical errors in deploying his troops. Unwilling to bet decisively on whether Howe would attack Manhattan Island directly or attempt to take Long Island first,

Washington spread his troops between the two locales. Even after word arrived in late August that British troops had landed at Gravesend Bay, near modern-day Coney Island, Washington clung to the idea that the landing on Long Island was a mere feint, and that a direct attack on Manhattan might still be Howe's true plan.

Washington did, however, send additional regiments to guard the roads that led through the Heights of Gowan—at Bedford, Flatbush, and Gowanus. Each of those roads was so narrow and well protected that any attempt to thread the British forces through would result in heavy losses for Howe. But Howe did not have his eye on those more direct routes to Brooklyn. Instead he sent the vast majority of his troops all the way around to the farthest point of the Heights, to the Jamaica Pass, in one of the great flanking moves of military history. In doing so, he exploited to deadly effect the most egregious mistake of Washington's entire career. While Washington had dispatched thousands of troops to guard the other three roads, only five sentries were planted near a lonely establishment named the Rising Sun Tavern at the entrance to the Jamaica Pass. The five men were captured without so much as a single shot fired.

Once Howe moved his men through the rocky gorge, he was able to make a surprise assault on the rebel troops from the rear. While the Battle of Brooklyn raged on for another seventy-two hours, it was effectively over the moment Howe made it through the Jamaica Pass. Within two weeks, New York belonged to the British, though Washington did distinguish himself by plotting an overnight evacuation of all his ground forces from Brooklyn—shielded by a dense fog that had settled over the harbor—a move that managed to keep most of his army intact for the subsequent battles of the Revolutionary War. This is the great irony of the Battle of Brooklyn: Washington's most cunning decision came not in his defense of New York but in the quick confidence of his decision to give it up.

Washington's decisions were ultimately so flawed that the American side never really recovered from them, in that New York remained under British control until the end of the war. But, of course, Washington's side did ultimately win out over the British, and while Washington was never a brilliant military tactician, none of his subsequent decisions were as flawed as his botched attempt to hold on to the isle of Manhattan. Why did his decision-making powers fail him so miserably in the Battle of Brooklyn?

In his initial decision to defend the city, Washington appears to have suffered from a well-known psychological trait known as loss aversion. As countless studies have shown, humans are wired to resist losses more than to seek gains. There seems to be something in our innate mental toolbox that stubbornly refuses to give up something we possess, even if it's in our long-term best interest to do so. That desire to keep Manhattan may have led Washington to make one of the most elemental mistakes in military tactics: by leaving a significant portion of his troops behind on Manhattan, he ensured that the British would encounter a greatly diminished force in Brooklyn. His only real hope would have been in doubling down on a Brooklyn defense, but instead, unable to countenance the idea of leaving the crown jewel undefended, Washington hedged his bets.

The real mystery is why he left the Jamaica Pass so woefully undefended. Why bother going to the trouble of fortifying the roads that led to Brooklyn but still leave one wide open? The answer, it turns out, begins with a virus: several weeks before the British attack, General Greene succumbed to the "camp fever" that had been ravaging the American troops, and by August 20, his condition had deteriorated to the point that he had to be evacuated to the countryside north of the city. It was Greene who had made the most impassioned arguments that the British would attempt an all-out attack on Long Island—and, most crucially, it was Greene who possessed the most thorough knowledge of Long Island's geography. Had Greene been at Washington's side once it became clear that Howe's men were making their way toward Brooklyn, it seems impossible that the Jamaica Pass would have remained so vulnerable.

When Greene left Washington's inner circle to take to his sickbed, Washington's ability to perceive the conditions on the ground in Long Island was fundamentally compromised. This is a recurring theme in complex decisions: In trying to understand a problem with many interacting variables, it's often impossible for us to perceive all the relevant elements directly. So our decision is built out of proxies and translators, other specialized minds that report back to us with their assessment of the situation. Part of making the right decision is learning how to make sense of all those different inputs. But it is just as important to recognize the holes that have opened up in your network, the unreliable translators. Washington's army was blindsided by the British attack, but only because Washington himself seems to have been blind to the intelligence loss he suffered when Greene left his war council. It was not just that he couldn't see the geography of Long Island as clearly; it was that he failed to recognize how faulty his vision had become.

MAPS, MODELS, AND INFLUENCE DIAGRAMS

No one makes a hard decision without some kind of mental map. Sometimes those maps are literal ones. In the months after the discovery of the mysterious compound in Abbottabad, the National Geospatial-Intelligence Agency began translating its satellite surveillance of the building and its grounds into a 3-D computer model. Eventually, based on that analysis, they built a physical model that was the size of a card table, with detailed representations of the walls, windows, and trees. (They even included a toy car representing al-Kuwaiti's white jeep.) The model turned out to be a productive tool in wrestling with the question of who was living in the compound, and ultimately proved to be essential to the decision of how to infiltrate the space—though, as we will see, it failed to account for one key variable, an omission that almost doomed the operation.

Sometimes the maps are more metaphoric: In our minds, we build on a model of the situation that confronts us, and all its threadlike pressures. Often it is a bit of both. A jury decision at a murder trial might involve a physical map of the crime scene and a metaphoric map of all the other evidence to be considered. A decision to release a new product could include a map of all the regions where it might potentially sell, as well as a metaphoric map of the complexities involved in producing the product in the first place.

Mapping the terrain of a hard choice is usually the first step we take in making a decision. We chart the participants who will be involved in the decision and its aftermath—in Washington's case, the rival military forces of the British and Revolutionary armies. We model the physical or situational forces that shape the interactions between the participants: the topography of Long Island and Manhattan, the weather, the range of the cannons at Fort Clinton. We take stock of the mental or emotional states that will likely shape the behavior of the key players: the fading morale of the underpaid and ill-prepared American troops, the willingness of General Howe to make a surprise attack. With hard choices, these maps almost by definition must be full spectrum in their scope. Washington's choice required that he consider the individual psychology of Howe, the collective emotional state of his men, the technological prowess of the weapons under his possession, the growing physical threat from the camp fever that had felled Nathanael Greene, the mandate to protect New York delivered to him by the Continental Congress, the financial pressures of a military force with no sovereign power wealthy enough to fund it, and the broader historical currents of the conflict between the former colonies and England itself.

Washington's choice at the Battle of Brooklyn had a magnitude that most group decisions rarely possess: There were thousands of lives at stake, not to mention the precarious life of a new nation. But the mental map he had to construct was not so different from the kind of map we build in our heads when confronting more mundane decisions. They are both trying to model multivariable systems across the full spectrum of experience, ranging from the inner emotional life of our colleagues to the geography of the community that surrounds us, and from our political worldview or religious beliefs to the mundane realities of financial limitations or opportunities. Like any form of navigation, the best way to start on the journey of a hard choice is to have a good map as your guide. But mapping is not the same as deciding. What the map should ultimately reveal is a set of potential paths, given the variables at play in the overall system. Figuring out *which* path to take requires other tools.

In this sense, mapping is the point in the decision process where divergence and diversity are key. You are not looking for consensus in this phase; you are looking to expand the range of possible factors (and, ultimately, decision paths). The challenge of mapping is getting outside our intuitive sense of the situation in front of us. Our minds naturally gravitate to narrowband interpretations, compressing the full spectrum down into one dominant slice. Cognitive scientists sometimes call this anchoring. When facing a decision that involves multiple, independent variables, people have a tendency to pick one "anchor" variable and make their decision based on that element. The anchors vary depending on the values you bring to the decision: in the aisles of a grocery store, some shoppers anchor on price, others on known brands, others on nutritional value, others on environmental impact. Compressing the spectrum turns out to be a perfectively adaptive strategy in a world characterized by an abundance of microchoices. You don't want to build a complex, full-spectrum map for every item you buy at the supermarket. But for decisions that may reverberate for years, it makes sense to expand our perspective.

Decision theorists have developed a tool for sketching out these kinds of full-spectrum choices: *influence diagrams*. Diagramming a complex decision using these visual tools can help elucidate the true complexity of the issue. Influence diagrams are widely used in environmental-impact studies, precisely the kind of analysis that was so sorely lacking in the decision to fill Collect Pond. They help us visualize the chain of effects—sometimes called impact pathways—that inevitably follow hard choices.

Imagine a group of time-traveling environmental planners had arrived in Manhattan circa 1800 and sketched out an influence diagram of the dilemma the city faced in its debate over the future of Collect Pond. A simple version would have probably looked something like this:

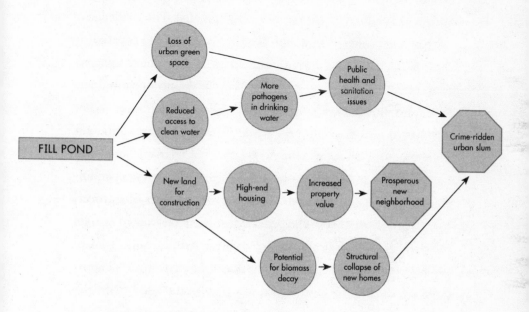

Note how even a simple diagram like this shows the connections that link a wide range of factors: from biological microorganisms to real estate markets, from disease outbreaks to the structural failure of buildings. Without a clear vision of the future effects that would ripple out from the decision to fill the pond, the decision might seem to be a clear choice between two competing value systems: pro-nature versus pro-economic development. You can have a lovely park with clean water and wildlife enjoying a natural oasis in the middle of the bustling city, or you can fill in the pond and create new housing stock to shelter the city's growing population, making some money for the real estate developers along the way. But the impact pathways rarely run in straight lines. The destruction of Collect Pond might create a short-term economic boost with the construction of new housing, but long-term, the creation of a park might result in more economic benefit, as the price of an apartment on Central Park West will testify.

No one bothered to sketch out an influence diagram before the city filled in Collect Pond, because we simply didn't have the conceptual tools to imagine the decision in those terms two centuries ago. But today we do, and those tools are used every day in planning decisions around the world, with material benefits that we rarely pause to appreciate.

Just a few miles northeast of Jamaica Pass, not far from the present-day neighborhood of Jamaica, Queens, the largest lake in all of New York City—known as Meadow Lake—lies between the parallel arteries of the Grand Central Parkway and the Van Wyck Expressway. Originally a salt marsh, the lake took its modern form during the construction of the 1939 World's Fair, but in recent decades, during warm months of the year, a thick coating of yellow-green algae covered the lake, depleting oxygen levels and posing health risks to both fish and humans interacting with the water. In 2014, inspired by their success at revitalizing the rivers that surround Manhattan island, a group of city and state agencies decided to turn their focus to the city's lakes. Restoring Meadow Lake to conditions that would be healthy for both wildlife and human recreation forced them to sketch out the impact pathways that had created the algae bloom in the first place and to contemplate the potential effects of making changes to those pathways. They discovered that a 1992 EPA regulation had

compelled the city to add phosphate to the drinking water—
some of which fed Meadow Lake—in an effort to reduce the lead
levels in the city's water supply. The phosphate functioned as a
key nutrient supporting the algae superbloom on the lake's surface. Storm-water runoff from nearby highways was also bringing
nitrogen into the lake, accelerating the bloom. Even coal from
nearby barbecues was finding its way into the water.

In the end, the city decided to filter out those algae-supporting
nutrients by restoring part of the lake to its original form, with
wetlands plants lining the eastern shore and serving as a natural
filtration system that removes the phosphates and nitrogen before
they can fuel the algae superbloom. (The city also built a land-
scaped "bioswale" that collects the highway runoff before it
reaches the lake.) The result has been a transformed habitat for
both human recreation and for the formerly oxygen-starved fish
that swim in the lake. Just a few years ago, a new boat-rental con-
cession opened on the northern edge of the lake, and today you
can see New Yorkers kayaking and enjoying paddleboat rides on
clear water all summer long.

Restoring Meadow Lake required a full-spectrum map to
make sense of the problem and to decide on a path for solving it.
It forced the planners to think on the scale of individual mole-
cules of nitrogen and phosphate. It forced them to think about
the nutrient cycles of blue-green algae, the oxygen needs of fish
swimming in the lake, the transportation corridors of urban
highways, and the casual pollution caused by human beings grill-
ing burgers on a summer weekend. It was a complicated map to
draw, but not an impossible one. And it was the kind of map that
would have been unthinkable just a few decades ago. You can be
sure Robert Moses wasn't thinking about blue-green algae and

nitrogen runoff when he was building Grand Central Parkway and the Van Wyck. Today we *can* make maps with that full-spectrum sensitivity to the system we are altering. Those kayakers on Meadow Lake are likely unaware of this advance; all they know is that the water looks a lot cleaner than it did a few years ago. But behind that surface transformation lies a much more profound advance in our ability to make farsighted decisions in environmental planning. We make better decisions because we can see across a much wider spectrum.

DIVERSITY

Every farsighted decision has its own unique map, of course, and the art of making those choices with as much wisdom as possible lies not in forcing that map to match some existing template, but instead in developing the kind of keen vision required to see the situation as it truly is. And the best way to develop that vision is to get different pairs of eyes on the problem.

A few years ago, the water authority in the Greater Vancouver region faced a decision not unlike the one that confronted the citizens of New York two hundred years ago as to the fate of Collect Pond. A growing urban population meant that the region's existing freshwater sources were not going to be able to meet demand in the coming years. New sources would have to be tapped, with inevitable impact on local environment, commerce, and communities. The city's home in the rainy Pacific Northwest gave it the luxury of many potential options: three reservoirs could be expanded, new pipelines could be built to a number of distant lakes, or wellfields could be drilled along one prominent river. Like filling or preserving Collect Pond, this was a decision whose consequences would likely persist for more than a century. (Water from the Capilano River, for instance, was first delivered to Vancouver residents in the late 1800s, and continues to be a major water source for the city.) But this decision began with an earnest attempt to model all the important variables from a full-spectrum perspective. It built that model by consulting a wide range of stakeholders, each contributing a different perspective on the problem at hand: local residents living near each of the water sources being considered; indigenous people with sacred ties to the land being surveyed; environmental activists and conservationists; health and water-safety regulators; even local citizens who used the various bodies of water for boating, fishing, or other water sports. Stakeholders evaluated each option for its impact on a wide range of variables: "aquatic habitat, terrestrial habitat, air quality, visual quality, employment, recreation, traffic and noise, and property values."

The approach taken by the Vancouver Water Authority has become commonplace in many important land use and environmental planning deliberations. The techniques used to bring those different voices together vary depending on the methodologies embraced by the planners (or the consultants they have hired to help run the process). But they share a core attribute: a recognition that mapping a decision as complex as establishing new sources of drinking water for a metropolitan center requires a network of diverse perspectives to generate anything resembling an accurate map of the problem. The most common term for this kind of collaborative deliberation is a "charrette." The word derives from the French word for wagon; apparently architecture students at the École des Beaux-Arts in the 1800s would deposit their scale models and drawings in a small wagon that would be wheeled out to collect student submissions as the deadline for a project approached. Students making last-minute tweaks to their projects were said to be working *en charrette*—adding the finishes touches as the wagon made its rounds. In its modern usage, though, the design charrette does not refer to a last-minute cram session, but rather to an open, deliberative process where different stakeholders are invited to critique an existing plan, or suggest new potential ideas for the space or resource in question. The charrette makes it harder for a complex decision to be evaluated purely from the narrowband perspective of a single business group or government agency.

One way in which charrettes differ from the more traditional forum of a community board meeting is that they conventionally take the form of a series of small-group meetings, not one large gathering. Keeping the groups separate reduces the potential for open conflict between groups that have competing values, of course, but it also generates a more diverse supply of ideas and assessments in the long run. "To derive the most useful information from multiple sources of evidence," Daniel Kahneman advises, "you should always try to make these sources independent of each other. This rule is part of good police procedure. When there are multiple witnesses to an event, they are not allowed to discuss it before giving their testimony. The goal is not only to prevent collusion by hostile witnesses, it is also to prevent unbiased witnesses from influencing each other." In situations where small-group separation is not possible, Kahneman suggests using another technique to preserve the full range of potential ideas: "Before an issue is discussed, all members of the committee should be asked to write a very brief summary of their position. This procedure makes good use of the value of the diversity of knowledge and opinion in the group. The standard practice of open discussion gives too much weight to the opinions of those who speak early and assertively, causing others to line up behind them."

In fact, the practical applications of "group" decision-making can sometimes be usefully broken down into a series of individual consultations. As legal scholar Cass Sunstein and others have observed, groups often possess a rich mix of information distributed among their members, but when they actually gather together in person, they tend to focus on *shared* information. As Sunstein writes:

> *Some group members are* cognitively central, *in the sense that their personal knowledge is also held by many other group members. What the cognitively central members know, other people know as well. A cognitively central group member is thus defined as one who possesses information in common with all or most group members. By contrast, other group members are* cognitively peripheral; *their own information is uniquely held. What they know is known by no one else, and what they may know might be really important. For that very reason, well-functioning groups need to take advantage of cognitively peripheral people. These people are especially significant. But in most groups, cognitively central people have a disproportionate influence in discussion and participate more in group deliberations. By contrast, cognitively peripheral people end up having little influence and participate less, often to the group's detriment.*

Something about the bonding environment of a face-to-face meeting seems to elicit a borderline unconscious response in humans to discuss elements that are commonly known to other members of the group, either because individuals like the feeling of consensus, or because they worry about being perceived as some kind of outsider if they reveal information not shared by most of the other members. If you don't design the decision process to expose this crucial unshared information—the technical term for it, coined by the psychologists Garold Stasser and William Titus, is *hidden profiles*—the primary benefit of consulting with a wide range of people will be lost. In the divergent stage of a decision, the stage where you're trying to assemble the most full-spectrum map of the situation at hand, the best approach may well be a series of interviews with individuals, not a team meeting. In those one-on-one conversations, the power of the "cognitively central" in-group disappears; people just know what they know, and thus are more likely to share that valuable piece of information unknown to the rest of the group.

Whether you build your map through a series of small group sessions or individual interviews, the most important element is the *diversity* of perspectives you assemble. The very act of diversifying the group clearly improves its decision-making abilities. The power of diversity is so strong that it appears to apply even when the diverse perspectives being added to the group have no relevant expertise to the case at hand. When the Vancouver Water Authority assembled its network of stakeholders to help make the decision about new sources of drinking water, it was laudable that they integrated feedback from stakeholders like water sports enthusiasts and indigenous peoples. But they would have also been able to improve their decision-making process simply by inviting feedback from random people who had no connection to Vancouver—as long as the backgrounds and expertise of those newcomers differed significantly from the original decision-makers at the water authority itself. Just the *presence* of difference appears to make a difference.

The connection between diversity and improvements in the collective IQ of a group has been demonstrated by hundreds of experiments over the past few decades. The social scientist Scott E. Page refers to this as the "diversity trumps ability" theory of group decision-making. But the way in which the presence of diverse viewpoints improves our judgment turns out to be more complicated than one would initially suspect. The conventional assumption was that newcomers to a previously homogeneous group improved the overall intelligence by bringing new ideas or values to the discussion, and indeed, in some cases, that kind of outside perspective did improve the group's overall intellect. But a number of studies have shown that the addition of "outsiders" to a homogeneous group also helps the "insiders" come up with more nuanced and original insights on their own.

A number of these studies revolve around simulated versions of one of the most important public decisions any of us will ever make: jury verdicts. About a decade ago, the social psychologist Samuel Sommers conducted a series of mock trials in which a jury debated and evaluated evidence from a sexual assault case. Some of the juries were entirely white, while other juries were more diverse in their racial makeup. By almost every important metric, the racially mixed juries performed better at their task. They considered more potential interpretations of the evidence, they remembered information about the case more accurately, and they engaged in the deliberation process with more rigor and persistence. Homogeneous groups—whether they are united by ethnic background, gender, or some other worldview like politics—tend to come to decisions too quickly. They settle early on a most-likely scenario, and don't spend the energy to question their assumptions, since everyone at the table seems to agree with the broad outline of the interpretation. But Sommers found that the mere presence of non-whites in the jury room made the white jurors more contemplative and open to other possible interpretations. Just the idea that there were diverse perspectives in the room helped the group build more accurate maps.

You can enhance the diversity of an existing group—without bringing in outsiders—simply by designating "expert roles" to each of the participants based on the knowledge they happen to bring to the discussion. A team of psychologists at Miami University conducted their own murder-mystery experiment in the 1990s that recruited college students to participate in a series of three-person mock investigations of a crime. Control groups in the experiment were given all the relevant clues required to correctly identify the perpetrator. In these group decisions, there was no unshared information. Each individual in the group had access to all the information required to crack the case. Not surprisingly, those teams made for successful detectives, identifying the correct suspect 70 percent of the time. In the other groups, hidden profiles were introduced: each team member had unshared information about one of the potential suspects, information that was not possessed by other members of the team. When those groups deliberated without any guidance as to their roles in the investigation, their detective skills deteriorated dramatically: they identified the correct suspect only a third of the time. But when each team member was specifically informed that they possessed knowledge about one of the suspects—that they were, in effect, an expert on Miss Marple or Professor Plum—their sleuthing improved to the point where they were almost indistinguishable from the control group that possessed all the information from the outset. By defining expertise, the scientists had subtly altered the group dynamics of the decision: instead of looking for the common ground of shared knowledge, the participants were empowered to share their unique perspective on the choice.

Introducing expert roles turns out to be a particularly effective technique in addressing the challenges of full-spectrum thinking, because in many cases the different bands or layers of the full-spectrum perspective correspond to different fields of expertise. In a formal hearing like a design charrette or the Vancouver water review, those expert roles may be relatively intuitive ones: the economist is there to talk about the economic impact of developing a reservoir in one community; the environmental scientist is there to talk about the environmental impact. But in less formal group deliberation, the different kinds of expertise in the room can easily remain unacknowledged, making it more likely that hidden profiles will remain hidden.

THE CONE OF UNCERTAINTY

In 2008, management professor Katherine Phillips led a decision-making study that replaced the mock trial format with a framework that was closer to *CSI* than *12 Angry Men*. Participants were asked to evaluate a collection of interviews from a detective's investigation of a homicide and decide, based on that assessment, which of several suspects actually committed the crime. Predictably enough, the introduction of outsiders made the teams better detectives, more attentive to the clues and more willing to share their own hidden profiles. But Phillips and her team discovered an additional, seemingly counterintuitive finding, one that has since become a key assumption in the science of decision-making (and, as we will see, of prediction). While the diverse groups were better detectives—they identified the correct subject more frequently than their homogeneous equivalents— they were also far less *confident* in the decisions they made. They were both more likely to be right and, at the same time, more open to the idea that they might be wrong. That might seem to be a paradox, but there turns out to be a strong correlation between astute decision-making and a willingness to recognize— and even embrace—uncertainty. Phillips's findings echo the famous Dunning-Kruger effect from cognitive psychology, in which low-ability individuals have a tendency to overestimate their skills. Sometimes the easiest way to be wrong is to be certain you are right.

If you have read a reasonable amount of the recent popular literature on decision-making or intuition, you are already well acquainted with the Tale of the Fire Commander and the Basement Fire. The story appeared originally in the 1999 book *Sources of Power*, written by the research psychologist Gary Klein, but it entered into the popular consciousness a few years later when Malcolm Gladwell featured it in his mega-bestseller *Blink*. Klein had spent many years exploring what he called "naturalistic decision-making"—breaking from the long-standing tradition of studying people's mental routines through clever lab experiments, and instead observing people making decisions, particularly decisions that involved intense time pressures, out in the real world. He spent a long stretch of time traveling with firefighters in Dayton, Ohio, watching them respond to emergencies, and also interviewing them about past decisions. One commander told Klein a story about what had initially appeared to be a relatively straightforward blaze in a single-story suburban home. Flames had been reported in the kitchen, near the back of the house, and so the commander brought his men to the kitchen, where they tried to subdue the fire. But quickly the situation began to confound the commander's expectations: it proved harder to extinguish the flames, and the house seemed both hotter and quieter than he would have normally expected with a fire of that scale. In a flash, he ordered his men to leave the building. Seconds later, the floor collapsed. A much larger fire had been burning in the basement all along. In his original account, Klein described the commander's thinking as follows:

> *The whole pattern did not fit right. His expectations were violated, and he realized he did not quite know what was going on. That was why he ordered his men out of the building. With hindsight, the reasons for the mismatch were clear. Because the fire was under him and not in the kitchen, it was not affected by his crew's attack, the rising heat was much greater than he had expected, and the floor acted like a baffle to muffle the noise, resulting in a hot but quiet environment.*

For Klein, the mysterious basement fire is a parable of sorts, illustrating the power of what he came to call "recognition-primed decision-making." Over years on the job, the Dayton commander had accumulated enough wisdom about how fires behaved that he was able to make a snap assessment of a novel situation, without being fully conscious of *why* he was making that assessment. It was a gut decision, but one that was primed by countless hours fighting fires in the past. But compare Klein's original account to the retelling that appears in Malcolm Gladwell's book. In Gladwell's hands, the story becomes an argument not just for the surprising power of "blink" judgments but also a cautionary tale about the cost of overthinking:

> *The fireman's internal computer effortlessly and instantly found a pattern in the chaos. But surely the most striking fact about that day is how close it all came to disaster. Had the lieutenant stopped and discussed the situation with his men, had he said to them, let's talk this over and try to figure out what's going on, had he done, in other words, what we often think leaders are supposed to do to solve difficult problems, he might have destroyed his ability to jump to the insight that saved their lives.*

Gladwell is absolutely correct that holding a planning charrette in the middle of the inferno would have been a disastrous strategy for fighting the fire. In situations that involve intense time pressure, gut instincts—shaped by experience—are inevitably going to play an important role. *Our* concern, of course, is with decisions that by definition do not involve such intense time restrictions, decisions where we have the luxury of not being slaves to our intuitive assessments because our deliberation time is weeks or months, not seconds. But there is still an important lesson for us in Klein's parable of the basement fire. Note the two different ways Klein and Gladwell describe the fateful decision point in the kitchen. In Klein's account, the signal moment comes when the fire chief "realized he did not quite know what was going on." But by Gladwell's retelling of the story, the moment takes on a different aspect: "The fireman . . . instantly found a pattern in the chaos." In Klein's original account, the fireman *doesn't* correctly diagnosis the situation, and he *doesn't* hit upon a brilliant strategy for fighting the fire. Instead, he literally runs away from the problem. (As he should have, given the situation.) In Gladwell's hands, the commander has an "insight that saved . . . lives."

There is no contesting the premise that the commander saved lives with his actions. The question is whether he had an "insight." To me, the parable of the basement fire teaches us how important it is to be aware of our blind spots, to recognize the elements of a situation that we *don't* understand. The commander's many years of experience fighting fires didn't prime him to perceive the hidden truth of the basement fire; it simply allowed him to recognize that he was missing something. And that recognition was enough to compel him to retreat from the building until he had a better understanding of what was going on.

Years ago, former secretary of defense Donald Rumsfeld was widely mocked for talking about the "known unknowns" of the Iraq War during a press conference, but the concept he was alluding to is actually a critical one in complex decision-making. There is wisdom in building an accurate mental map of the system you are trying to navigate, but there is also a crucial kind of wisdom in identifying the blank spots on the map, the places where you don't have clarity, either because you don't have the right set of stakeholders advising you (as Washington experienced with the loss of Nathanael Greene) or because some element of the situation is fundamentally unknowable.

Complex situations can present very different kinds of uncertainty. Several years ago, the scholars Helen Regan, Mark Colyvan, and Mark Burgman published an essay that attempted to classify all the variations of uncertainty that might confront an environmental planning project, like the Vancouver Water Authority review or the decision to fill Collect Pond. They came up with thirteen distinct species: measurement error, systematic error, natural variation, inherent randomness, model uncertainty, subjective judgment, linguistic uncertainty, numerical vagueness, nonnumerical vagueness, context dependence, ambiguity, indeterminacy in theoretical terms, and underspecificity. For nonspecialists, however, there are three primary forms that uncertainty can take, each with different challenges—and opportunities. Borrowing from Donald Rumsfeld, you can think of them as knowable unknowns, inaccessible unknowns, and unknowable unknowns. There are uncertainties that arise from some failure in our attempt to map the situation, failures that can be remedied by building better maps. Washington's incomplete understanding of the geography of Long Island falls into that category; had he been able to consult with Nathanael Greene during the crucial days leading up to the British assault, he would almost certainly have had a clearer map of the possible routes that Howe might take. There are uncertainties that involve information that exists but, for whatever reason, is inaccessible to us. It was entirely apparent to Washington and his subordinates that General Howe was planning some kind of attack on New York, but the specific plans he was considering were inaccessible to the Americans, assuming they had no spies within the British forces. And finally, there are uncertainties that result from the inherent unpredictability of the system being analyzed. Even if Washington had assembled the most advanced team of advisors on the planet, he would not have been able to predict, more than twenty-four hours in advance, the unusual fog that formed on the morning he evacuated Brooklyn, given the crude state of the art in weather forecasting in 1776.

Recognizing and separating these different forms of uncertainty is an essential step in building an accurate map of a hard choice. We all suffer from a tendency to overvalue the importance of the variables of a given system that we do understand, and undervalue the elements that are opaque to us, for whatever reason. It's the old joke of the drunk looking for his keys under a streetlamp, far from where he actually dropped them, because "the light is better over here." For the knowable unknowns, the best strategy is to widen and diversify the team of advisors or stakeholders, to track down your General Greene and get a more accurate map of the terrain, or build a scale model of the compound based on satellite imaging. But it's also crucial to keep track of the stubborn blind spots—the places where uncertainty can't be reduced with better maps or scouts on the ground. Weather forecasters talk about the "cone of uncertainty" in tracking hurricanes. They map out the most likely path the storm is going to take, but they also prioritize a much wider range of potential paths, all of which are within the realm of possibility as well. That wider range is the cone of uncertainty, and weather organizations go to great lengths to remind everyone living inside that cone to take precautions, even if they are outside the most likely path. Mapping decisions requires a similar vigilance. You can't simply focus on the variables that you are confident about; you also need to acknowledge the blank spots, the known unknowns.

In a way, this embrace of uncertainty echoes the fundamental techniques of the scientific method, as Richard Feynman describes it in a famous passage from his book *The Meaning of It All*:

> *When the scientist tells you he does not know the answer, he is an ignorant man. When he tells you he has a hunch about how it is going to work, he is uncertain about it. When he is pretty sure of how it is going to work, and he tells you, "This is the way it's going to work, I'll bet," he still is in some doubt. And it is of paramount importance, in order to make progress, that we recognize this ignorance and this doubt. Because we have the doubt, we then propose looking in new directions for new ideas. The rate of the development of science is not the rate at which you make observations alone but, much more important, the rate at which you create new things to test. If we were not able or did not desire to look in any new direction, if we did not have a doubt or recognize ignorance, we would not get any new ideas.*

One of the defining properties of the decision process that led to the capture of bin Laden was its relentless focus on uncertainty levels. In many respects, this focus on uncertainty was a direct response to the WMD fiasco of the previous administration, where circumstantial evidence had led the intelligence community to what proved to be an irrationally high confidence that Saddam Hussein was actively working on nuclear and chemical weapons. With the bin Laden decision, at almost every stage of the process—from the first surveillance of the compound to the final planning of the raid itself—analysts were specifically asked to rate their level of confidence in the assessment they were presenting. In November 2010, a consensus had developed among the analysts that bin Laden was, in fact, likely to be residing in the compound, but when Leon Panetta polled the analysts and other CIA officials, certainty levels varied from 60 to 90 percent. Not surprisingly, the analysts claiming less certainty were career officers who had participated in the Iraq WMD investigation and knew firsthand how unknown variables can transform what seems like a slam-dunk case into a much murkier affair.

Asking people to rate their confidence level turns out to be a productive strategy on multiple levels, not just because it allows others to gauge how seriously to take their information, but because the very act of thinking about how certain you are about something makes you think about what you might be missing. It serves as a kind of antidote to the often fatal disease of overconfidence that plagues so many complex decisions. The decision process that led to bin Laden's death didn't stop at asking people to rate their uncertainty. The senior officials involved in the decision—from Panetta to John Brennan, Obama's counterterrorism advisor—stoked the coals of uncertainty by demanding that the analysts challenge their assumptions. In the early stages of the investigation, when so much hinged on the question of whether al-Kuwaiti was still directly connected to bin Laden, the agency analysts were asked to come up with alternate explanations for al-Kuwaiti's suspicious behavior—plausible scenarios that would *not* connect him to bin Laden. Analysts suggested that perhaps he had left al-Qaeda and was now working for some other criminal enterprise—a drug ring, perhaps—that might have had a need for a high-security compound. Others proposed that he had stolen money from the terrorist network and was using the compound for his own protection. In another scenario, al-Kuwaiti was still working for al-Qaeda, but the compound merely housed bin Laden's relatives, not the terrorist mastermind himself.

Over time, the agency shot down each of these alternate explanations and became increasingly convinced that the compound had some direct connection to al-Qaeda. But the analysts continued to have their assumptions challenged by their supervisors. As Peter Bergen writes:

> Brennan pushed them to come up with intelligence that disproved the notion that bin Laden was living in the Abbottabad compound, saying, "I'm tired of hearing why everything you see confirms your case. What we need to look for are the things that tell us what's not right about our theory. So what's not right about your inferences?" The analysts came back to the White House one day and started their intelligence update, saying, "Looks like there's a dog on the compound." Denis McDonough, Obama's deputy national security advisor, remembers thinking, "Oh, that's a bummer. You know, no self-respecting Muslim's gonna have a dog." Brennan, who had spent much of his career focused on the Middle East and spoke Arabic, pointed out that bin Laden, in fact, did have dogs when he was living in Sudan in the mid-1990s.

What began as an explicit search for contradictory evidence— evidence that might undermine the interpretation around which the group was slowly coalescing—turned out, in the end, to generate evidence that made that interpretation even stronger. Either way, the exercise forces you to see the situation with more clarity, to detect the whorls of the fingerprint with greater accuracy.

Challenging assumptions, seeking out contradictory evidence, ranking certainty levels—all these strategies serve the divergent stage of the decision process well, helping to expand the map, propose new explanations, and introduce new variables. The analysts in the intelligence agency had extensively reviewed the obvious variables that the compound mystery presented—the design of the structure, its geographic location, the information (or lack thereof) flowing in and out of the residence—but it took an extra step of probing uncertainty to get them to think about the pets on the property, which turned out to be an important clue. Of course, spending too much time probing uncertainty risks leaving you in a Hamlet-like limbo of indecisiveness. Amazon's Jeff Bezos famously adheres to a "70 percent rule" in making decisions that involve uncertainty: instead of waiting for total confidence in a choice—a confidence that may never arrive, given the nature of bounded rationality—Bezos pulls the trigger on decisions once he has reduced his uncertainty level to 30 percent. Instead of adopting the rational choice myth of perfect certainty, the 70 percent rule acknowledges that our vision is inevitably going to be somewhat blurry. By measuring the known unknowns and the blind spots, we avoid the pitfalls of simply trusting our initial instincts. But at the same time, the 70 percent threshold keeps us from the paralysis of requiring perfect clarity.

By the end of 2010, as the investigation into the compound's occupants continued, a second decision process opened up, this one revolving less around interpretation and more around action. Having decided that there was at least a reasonable likelihood that

Osama bin Laden had been located, President Obama and his advisors now had to decide what to do about it. This stage involved many of the elements that were crucial to the first stage: uncertainty levels were probed, diverse perspectives embraced. But the divergent explorations of this stage were searching for something fundamentally different this time around. They weren't just trying to uncover previously hidden clues that might explain the mystery of the Abbottabad compound. They were also now trying to uncover new options for getting to bin Laden himself. Part of the art of mapping a complex decision is creating a full-spectrum portrait of all the variables that might influence your choice. But part of that mapping process is also coming up with new choices.

THE UNDISCOVERED PATH

In the early 1980s, a business school professor at Ohio State named Paul Nutt set out to catalogue real-world decisions the way a botanist might catalog the various types of vegetation growing in a rain forest. Decision theorists had been talking about the phases of the decision process for years: identifying the choice, evaluating the options on the table, and so on. Nutt wanted to see how these abstract phases played out in the wild. In his initial study, published in 1984, he analyzed seventy-eight different decisions made by senior management at a range of public and private organizations in the United States and Canada: insurance companies, government agencies, hospitals, consulting firms. Nutt conducted extensive interviews with the participants to reconstruct each decision, and then cataloged each one using a preexisting taxonomy of decision phases. Some choices were made almost reflexively by looking to some historical precedent and simply adopting that proven strategy; others sought out active feedback on a proposed path, but never contemplated alternate paths. (Nutt called these "whether or not" decisions.) Some of the more sophisticated teams deliberated multiple choices and made some attempt to weigh their respective pros and cons.

The most striking finding in Nutt's research was this: Only 15 percent of the case studies involved a stage where the decision-makers actively sought out a new option beyond the initial choices on the table at the outset. In a later study, Nutt found that only 29 percent of organizational decisions contemplated more than one alternative at all. In their book *Decisive*, Dan and Chip Heath compare Nutt's study to one that found that teenagers make choices with almost the exact same limitations: only 30 percent of teenagers considered more than one alternative in confronting a personal choice in their lives. (As they put it, "most organizations seem to be using the same decision process as a hormone-crazed teenager.") Over the years, Nutt and other researchers have convincingly demonstrated a strong correlation between the number of alternatives deliberated and the ultimate success of the decision itself. In one of his studies, Nutt found that participants who considered only one alternative ultimately judged their decision a failure more than 50 percent of the time, while decisions that contemplated at least two alternatives were felt to be successes two-thirds of the time. If you find yourself mapping a "whether or not" question, you're almost always better off turning it into a "which one" question that gives you more available paths.

The search for additional options is yet another realm in which diversity proves to be a key asset. Having different perspectives on a problem not only sheds more light on all the factors that shape the decision; it also makes it easier to see previously unimagined alternatives. (This is one space in which the literature on innovation overlaps with the literature on decision-making: in both fields, diversity turns out to be key in widening the possibility space, generating new ideas.) What Nutt's research made clear was how important it is to deliberately carve out a phase of the decision process within which entirely new alternatives are explored, to resist the easy gravitational pull toward the initial framing of the decision, particularly if it happens to take the form of a "whether or not" single alternative.

If you do find yourself stuck with a single path decision, Chip and Dan Heath suggest an intriguing—and somewhat counterintuitive—thought experiment to get outside that limited perspective: deliberately reduce your options. If your organization seems to have settled into the comfortable assumption that Path A is the only route available to them, then imagine a world where Path A is roadblocked. What would you do then? "Removing options can in fact do people a favor," the Heath brothers write, "because it makes them notice that they're stuck on one small patch of a wide landscape." Think of the map of Brooklyn in 1775: Washington had mapped out two primary paths that the British might take in their assault on New York: a direct naval attack on lower Manhattan, and a land-based attack through the Heights of Gowan. But if he had gone through the mental exercise of taking those two options off the table, he might have been able to anticipate the flanking move through Jamaica Pass, even without the aid of Nathanael Greene.

OPTIMAL EXTREMISM

The stretch of Tenth Avenue running along Manhattan's West Side south of Thirty-Third Street used to be known as "Death Avenue," a tribute to the many pedestrians and vehicles that met their demise colliding with the New York Central freight trains that ran parallel to the street. In 1934, the railway moved to an elevated viaduct that carried goods from the manufacturing and meatpacking centers above Houston Street up to Midtown, carving its way through several buildings along the route. As Lower Manhattan lost its manufacturing base, the railway grew increasingly irrelevant. In 1980, a train with three boxcars porting frozen turkeys made the final run on the tracks.

In the two decades that followed, the viaduct was officially closed to public use, and in those vacant years, the rail lines were slowly reclaimed by nature: waist-high grasses and weeds rose between the ties. Graffiti artists covered the iron and concrete with spray-paint tags; at night, kids would sneak up onto the tracks to drink beer or smoke pot, and enjoy this strange parallel universe thirty feet above the bustling streets of Chelsea. But for most of the "official community" that surrounded the train line, the viaduct was an eyesore and, worse, a threat to public safety. A group of local business owners sued the line's owner, Conrail, to have the viaduct removed. In 1992, the Interstate Commerce Commission sided with the business group and decreed that the tracks had to be demolished. For ten years a debate raged over who would pay for the demolition.

And then something surprising happened. At a community meeting, a painter named Robert Hammond and a writer named

Joshua David happened to strike up a conversation and began tossing around ideas for revitalizing the elevated tracks—not as a transportation platform but as a park. The idea was dismissed as fanciful by the Giuliani administration when it was first proposed, but rapidly gathered momentum. A photographer named Joel Sternfeld took a series of haunting photographs of the abandoned tracks, the rogue grasses shimmering between them like some kind of wheat field transported from the Great Plains into postindustrial Manhattan. Within a few years the plan had the blessing of the visionary head of parks under Mayor Bloomberg, Amanda Burden, and a public-private partnership raised millions to support the transformation. By the end of the decade, the first stretch of the High Line Park was open to the public: one of the most inventive and widely admired twenty-first-century urban parks built anywhere in the world, and a major new tourist attraction for New York City.

The High Line was not a natural resource like Collect Pond, but the basic outline of its history is not dissimilar: an urban resource that once served a vital function for the city's population, now rendered impractical and even dangerous thanks to neglect and the shifting industrial activities of a growing city. But the way the city ultimately wrestled with the decision of what to do with this derelict structure turned out to be much more creative than the choice to fill Collect Pond. For a decade, the decision was framed entirely in terms of an inevitable demolition. It was a classic "whether or not" decision. The structure was obviously useless—freight trains were not returning to Lower Manhattan—and so the only real question was how to get rid of it. Was it the city's responsibility or was it Conrail's? But lurking in that binary choice was a hidden third option, one that forced the participants to think about the viaduct in an entirely new way. Seen from street level, the High Line was an obvious eyesore. But seen from the tracks itself, it offered a captivating new perspective on the city around it.

We have already seen how doubt and uncertainty need to be actively confronted in making a hard choice. But often the most essential form of doubt involves questioning the options that appear to be on the table. Making complex decisions is not just about mapping the terrain that will influence each choice. It's also, as Paul Nutt's research made clear, a matter of discovering new choices. This is the definitional myopia of pros-vs.-cons lists like the one Darwin sketched out in his journal before getting married. When you sit down to tabulate the arguments for and against a particular decision, you have already limited the potential range of options to two paths: get married, or don't get married. But what if there are other, more inventive ways of reaching our objectives or satisfying the conflicting needs of the stakeholders? Maybe it's not a choice between tearing the viaduct down or letting it continue as a dangerous ruin. Maybe it could be reinvented?

The challenge, of course, is how you trick your mind into perceiving that third option, or the fourth and fifth options lurking somewhere behind it. The multidisciplinary structure of the charrette can certainly help with this. Other stakeholders in the situation are likely to perceive options that you might not naturally hit upon, given the narrow bands of your own individual perspective. Reducing your options as a thought experiment, as Chip and Dan Heath suggest, can also be a useful strategy. But there's another way of thinking about this problem, one that connects directly to the kinds of decisions we wrestle with collectively in democratic societies. The first people to realize that the High Line might have a second act as a recreational space were not the establishment decision-makers of urban planning and local business groups. They were people living—and playing—at the margins of society: graffiti artists, trespassers looking for the thrill of partying in a forbidden space, urban adventurers seeking a different view of the city. In a very literal sense, those first High Line explorers occupied an extreme position in the debate over the High Line's future, in that they were occupying a space above the streets that almost no one else had bothered to experience. They were extreme and marginal both in the sense of their social identities and lifestyle choices, and in the sense of where they were standing. And even when the idea for a park emerged among more traditional sources, it was not a city planner or business leader who first proposed it—it was instead a writer, a painter, and a photographer.

Extremism is not only a potential defense of liberty; it's also often the source of new ideas and decision paths that aren't visible to the mainstream. Most significant social change first takes the form of an "extreme" position, far from the centrist fifty-yard-line of conventional wisdom. A society where extreme positions are not granted a meaningful voice is a society incapable of fundamental change. Universal suffrage, climate change, gay marriage, marijuana legalization—these are all ideas that came into the world as "extremist" positions, far from the mainstream. But over time they found their way into supra-majority-level consensus. It was an extreme position in 1880 to suggest that women should vote, but now the idea of a male-only electorate seems absurd to all but the most unrepentant sexist. Of course, there are many extreme positions that turn out to be dead-ends, or worse: 9/11 deniers and white supremacists are also extremists in the current political spectrum. But we are far less likely to stumble across truly inventive new paths—in civic life as in urban parks—if we mute all the extreme voices in the mix.

DOWNSTREAM

Outsiders are not the only ones who can reveal previously unimagined options. Sometimes the new pathways get discovered by those at the top of the chain. As president, Barack Obama apparently had a gift for discerning alternate choices. "Advisers had a way of narrowing the choice to option A or option B, and then steering the president to the one they preferred," Mark Bowden writes in his account of the bin Laden raid. "It was all in how the issue was framed. This method didn't have a chance with Obama. He would listen to A and B, ask a lot of good questions, and more often than not propose an entirely different course, option C, which seemed to emerge wholly formed from his head."

In the late winter of 2011, the bin Laden investigation switched from a decision about the identity of the compound's occupants to a decision about how best to attack the compound. No one knew for certain if the mysterious figure that had been observed pacing on the compound grounds—though always partially concealed from satellite view—was in fact the al-Qaeda mastermind, but the odds were good enough to justify some kind of military assault. The question was, what kind of assault? Initially, Obama had been presented with two options: a helicopter raid, where Special Ops forces might be able to kill or capture bin Laden without destroying the compound, or a B-2 bombing run, where thirty precision bombs would be dropped on the compound, destroying the structure and any underground tunnels beneath it. Neither option was ideal: the helicopter raid involved flying into Pakistani airspace without notifying the Pakistanis themselves, and had an unmistakable echo of Jimmy Carter's disastrous 1980 helicopter raid to rescue the Iranian hostages. The bombing run was far easier to execute, but would likely destroy many nearby homes with dozens of civilian casualties, and would immolate all of the potential evidence on the compound site—most important, the evidence that bin Laden himself had been killed.

Faced with those two options, each with its own distinct drawbacks, Obama pushed the team to look for other possibilities, just as they had been pushed to look for contradictory evidence in identifying the compound's residents. In the end, the team settled on four options: the B-2 bombing; the Special Ops raid; a drone strike that would use an experimental highly accurate guided missile to take out "the pacer" directly but do little collateral damage to the compound or the surrounding neighborhood; and a coordinated attack with the Pakistanis, which would eliminate the risk of flying through their airspace without their consent.

Having conducted a full-spectrum analysis of the compound itself and mapped the potential options that would allow them to attack the compound, Obama and his team then shifted gears. They were no longer collecting evidence about the situation on the ground in Abbottabad, exposing hidden profiles, charting potential paths. Their minds had turned to the *consequences* of the choices they faced. Each path suggested a series of possible futures, with downstream effects that could reverberate for years.

As in all farsighted decisions, the choice Obama and team confronted in the decision to go after bin Laden forced them to think rigorously about what would come next.

The metaphor of a decision map is a powerful one. In confronting a hard choice, you are trying to describe the literal and figurative terrain around you: taking inventory of all the forces at play; sketching out all the regions that are visible, and at least acknowledging the blind spots; charting the potential paths you can take in navigating the space. But, of course, in one respect, the concept of a decision map is misleading. Maps define the current lay of the land. They are, in a sense, frozen in time. Decisions, on the contrary, unfold over days, weeks, or years. Choosing the right path depends not just on our ability to understand the current state of the system but also our ability to *predict* what comes next. To make complex choices, you need a full-spectrum appraisal of the state of things and a comprehensive list of potential choices available to you. But you also need an informed model of how that state is likely to change based on the choice you eventually make. It may seem challenging to build a mental map of a complicated, multivariable system. But it's even harder to predict the future.

2

PREDICTING

Let him start for the Continent, then, without our pronouncing on his future. Among all forms of mistake, prophecy is the most gratuitous.

・GEORGE ELIOT, *MIDDLEMARCH*

For most of its history, the science of brain function had a grim reliance on catastrophic injuries. Scientists had been dissecting brains for centuries, but until modern neuro-imaging tools like PET and fMRI allowed us to track blood flow to different parts of the brain in real time, it was extremely difficult to tell which parts of the brain were responsible for different mental states. Most of our understanding of brain specialization was based on case studies like that of Phineas Gage, the nineteenth-century railroad worker who somehow survived an iron rod piercing his left frontal lobe and went on to display a striking set of changes in his personality. Before neuro-imaging, if you wanted to ascertain the function of a specific part of the brain, you found someone who had lost that part in some terrible accident, and you figured out how the injury had impaired them. If they were blind, the injury must have impacted their visual system; if they had amnesia, the damaged area must have something to do with memory.

This was an extremely inefficient way to study the human brain, so when PET and fMRI arrived in the 1970s and 1980s, bringing the promise of studying healthy brains at work, neuroscientists were understandably thrilled at the prospect. But scientists quickly realized that the new technologies required a baseline state for their scans to be meaningful. Blood, after all, is circulating through the entire brain all the time, so what you are looking for in a PET or fMRI are *changes* in that blood flow: a surge of activity in one area, a decrease in another. When you see a surge in the auditory cortex as a Bach sonata plays in the fMRI room, the scan makes it clear that that specific part of the temporal lobe plays a role in listening to music. But to see that surge, you have to be able to contrast it to a resting state. It's only by tracking the differences between different states—and their different patterns of blood flow throughout the brain—that the scans become useful.

For years, scientists assumed this wasn't all that tricky. You put your research subjects into the scanner, asked them to rest and do nothing, and then asked them to do whatever task you were studying: listening to music, speaking, playing chess. You scanned their brains while they were resting and then scanned them again when they were active, and the computer analyzed the differences and conjured up an image that foregrounded the changes in blood flow, not unlike a modern weather map that shows you the different intensities of a storm system approaching a metro area. In the mid-nineties, a brain researcher at the University of Iowa named Nancy Andreasen was conducting an experiment on memory using PET machines when she noticed something unusual in the results. The "rest" state scans didn't seem to show a decrease in activity. On the contrary—telling her subjects to sit still and not try to do anything in particular seemed to trigger a very specific pattern of active stimulation in their brains. In a paper published in 1995, Andreasen noted one additional detail about that pattern: the systems of the brain that lit up in the rest state were systems that are far less developed in the brains of non-human primates. "Apparently, when the brain/ mind thinks in a free and unencumbered fashion," Andreasen speculated, "it uses its most human and complex parts."

Soon a number of other researchers began exploring this strange behavior. In many studies, the brain turned out to be *more* active at rest than it was when it was supposedly being active. Before long, scientists began calling this recurring pattern of activity the "default network." In 1999, a team of researchers at the Medical College of Wisconsin led by J. R. Binder published an influential paper that suggested the default network involved "retrieval of information from long-term memory, information representation in conscious awareness in the form of mental images and thoughts, and manipulation of this information for problem-solving and planning." In other words, when we are left to our own mental devices, the mind drifts into a state where it swirls together memories and projections, mulls problems, and concocts strategies for the future. Binder went on to speculate on the adaptive value of this kind of mental activity. "By storing, retrieving, and manipulating internal information, we organize what could not be organized during stimulus presentation, solve problems that require computation over long periods of time, and create effective plans governing behavior in the future. These capabilities have surely made no small contribution to human survival and the invention of technology."

There is a simpler—and less revelatory—way of describing these discoveries: human beings daydream. We didn't need an fMRI scanner to find this out about ourselves. What the technology *did* reveal was just how much energy daydreaming required. What feels like the mind drifting off into reverie is actually, on the level of neural activity, a full workout. And the brain regions involved in that workout happen to be ones that are uniquely human. Why would our brains devote so many resources to something as innocuous and seemingly unproductive as daydreaming? This mystery has compelled another group of researchers to investigate what exactly we are thinking about when we daydream. An elaborate recent study by the social psychologist Roy Baumeister pinged five hundred people in Chicago at random points during the day and asked them what they were thinking about at that exact moment. If they weren't actively involved in a specific task, Baumeister found they were surprisingly likely to be thinking about the future, imagining events and emotions that, technically speaking, hadn't happened yet. They were three times more likely to be thinking about future events than about past events. (And even the past events they were ruminating on usually had some relevance for their future prospects.) If you take a step back and think about this finding, there is something puzzling about it. Human beings seem to spend a remarkable amount of time thinking about events that are by definition not real, that are figments of our imagination—because they haven't happened yet. This future orientation turns out to be a defining characteristic of the brain's default network.

When we let our mind wander, it naturally starts to run imagined scenarios about what lies ahead. We are not, as F. Scott Fitzgerald put it at the end of *The Great Gatsby*, boats against the current, borne back ceaselessly into the past. In fact, our minds tend to race ahead of the current, contemplating the future whenever they get the opportunity.

The psychologist Martin Seligman has argued recently that this capacity to build working hypotheses about future events—our ability to make long-term predictions that shape the decisions we make in life—may be the defining attribute of human intelligence. "What best distinguishes our species," he writes, "is an ability that scientists are just beginning to appreciate: We contemplate the future. Our singular foresight created civilization and sustains society. . . . A more apt name for our species would be *Homo prospectus*, because we thrive by considering our prospects. The power of prospection is what makes us wise. Looking into the future, consciously and unconsciously, is a central function of our large brain."

It is unclear whether non-human animals have any real concept of the future at all. Some organisms display behavior that suggests long-term forethought—like a squirrel burying a nut for winter—but those behaviors are all instinctive, shaped by genes, not cognition. The most advanced study of animal time schemes concluded that most animals can only plan ahead deliberately on the scale of minutes. Making decisions based on future prospects on the scale of months or years—even something as simple as planning a summer vacation in December—would be unimaginable even to our closest primate relatives. The truth is that we are constantly making predictions about events on the horizon, and those predictions steer the choices that we make in life.

Without that talent for prospection, we would be a fundamentally different species.

THE SUPERFORECASTERS

The fact that our brains evolved a default network that likes to ruminate on what might lie ahead of us does not necessarily mean that we are flawless at predicting future events, particularly when those events are full-spectrum affairs with long time horizons. A few decades ago, the political science professor Philip Tetlock famously conducted a series of forecasting tournaments, where pundits and public intellectuals were asked to make predictions about future events. Tetlock assembled a group of 284 "experts" from a broad range of institutions and political perspectives. Some were government officials, others worked for institutions like the World Bank, and some were public intellectuals who published frequently on the op-ed pages of major newspapers. Part of the brilliance of Tetlock's experiment is that he was trying to measure what author Stewart Brand called "the long view"—not the daily churn of the news cycle, but the slower, more momentous changes in society. Some forecasts involved events happening over the next year, but others asked participants to look forward over the coming decade. Most of the questions were geopolitical or economic in nature: Will a member of the European Union withdraw over the coming ten years? Will there be a recession in the United States in the next five years?

Tetlock collected 28,000 predictions over the course of his research and then took the momentous step that almost never accompanies the pronouncements of op-ed writers and cable news pundits: he actually compared the predictions to real-world outcomes and graded the forecasters for their comparative accuracy. As a kind of control, Tetlock compared the human forecasts to simple algorithmic versions, like "always predict no change" or "assume the current rate of change continues uninterrupted." If the forecast asked for the size of the US deficit in ten years, one algorithm would just answer, "The same as it is now." The other would calculate the rate at which the deficit was growing or shrinking and calculate the ten-year forecast accordingly.

The results, once Tetlock finished evaluating all the forecasts, were appallingly bad. Most so-called experts were no better than the figurative dart-throwing chimp. When asked to make predictions that looked at the longer-range trends, the experts actually performed *worse* than random guesses would have. The simplistic algorithmic forecasts ("present trends will continue") actually outperformed many of the experts, and Tetlock generally found that there was an inverse correlation between how well-known the expert was and the efficacy of their forecasts. The more media exposure you had, the less valuable your predictions were likely to be.

When Tetlock finally published these results in his 2009 book, *Expert Political Judgment*, they were widely reported in the news media, which was somewhat ironic, given that the lesson of Tetlock's study seemed to undermine the authority of media opinions. Yet Tetlock did uncover a statistically meaningful group of experts who were, in fact, better than the chimps, even at long-term forecasts. Their accuracy rates weren't anywhere near total clairvoyance, but there was something about them that was helping them see the long view more clearly than their peers. And so Tetlock turned to an even more interesting mystery:

What separated the successful forecasters from the charlatans? The usual suspects didn't pan out: it didn't make a difference if they had a PhD, or a higher IQ, or a post at a prestigious institution, or a higher level of security clearance. And it didn't really matter what their political beliefs were. "The critical factor," Tetlock writes, "was *how* they thought":

> One group tended to organize their thinking around Big Ideas, although they didn't agree on which Big Ideas were true or false. Some were environmental doomsters ("We're running out of everything"); others were cornucopian boomsters ("We can find cost-effective substitutes for everything"). Some were socialists (who favored state control of the commanding heights of the economy); others were free-market fundamentalists (who wanted to minimize regulation). As ideologically diverse as they were, they were united by the fact that their thinking was so ideological. They sought to squeeze complex problems into the preferred cause-effect templates and treated what did not fit as irrelevant distractions. . . . As a result, they were unusually confident and likelier to declare things "impossible" or "certain." . . . The other group consisted of more pragmatic experts who drew on many analytical tools, with the choice of tool hinging on the particular problem they faced. These experts gathered as much information from as many sources as they could. . . . They talked about possibilities and probabilities, not certainties. And while no one likes to say "I was wrong," these experts more readily admitted it and changed their minds.

Tetlock borrowed a metaphor from Isaiah Berlin's legendary line, which was itself cribbed from the ancient Greek poet

Archilochus—"The fox knows many things but the hedgehog knows one big thing"—and dubbed these two kinds of forecasters hedgehogs and foxes. In Tetlock's analysis, the foxes—attuned to a wide range of potential sources, willing to admit uncertainty, not devoted to an overarching theory—turned out to be significantly better at predicting future events than the more single-minded experts. The foxes were full spectrum; the hedgehogs were narrowband. When trying to make sense of a complex, shifting situation—a national economy, or technological developments like the invention of a computer—the unified perspective of a single field of expertise or worldview actually appears to make you *less* able to project future changes. For the long view, you need to draw on multiple sources for clues; dabblers and hobbyists outperform the unified thinkers.

Tetlock also noticed one other interesting trait about the successful forecasts—one drawn from the study of personality types instead of research methodology. Psychologists often refer to the "big five" traits that define the major axes of human personality: conscientiousness, extraversion, agreeableness, neuroticism, and openness to experience, which is also sometimes described as curiosity. When he evaluated his forecasters in terms of these basic categories, one jumped out: the successful forecasters as a group were much more likely to be open to experience. "Most people who are not from Ghana would find a question like 'Who will win the presidential election in Ghana?' pointless," Tetlock writes. "They wouldn't know where to start, or why to bother. But when I put that hypothetical question to [one of the successful forecasters] and asked for his reaction, he simply said, 'Well, here's an opportunity to learn something about Ghana.'"

But Tetlock's superforecasters were hardly prophets. As a

group they were roughly 20 percent better at predicting the future than the average hedgehog, which meant they only slightly outperformed chance. You could fill an entire library wing with histories of people who failed to see momentous developments coming, developments that with hindsight now seem obvious to us. Almost no one predicted the network-connected personal computer, for instance. Numerous science-fiction narratives—starting with H. G. Wells's vision of a "global brain"—imagined some kind of centralized, mechanical superintelligence that could be consulted for advice on humanity's biggest problems. But the idea of computers becoming effectively home appliances—cheap, portable, and employed for everyday tasks like reading advice columns or looking up sports scores—seems to have been almost completely inconceivable, even to the very people whose job it was to predict future developments in society! (The one exception was an obscure 1947 short story called "A Logic Named Joe" that features a device that not only closely resembles a modern PC but also includes functionality that anticipates Google queries as well.)

The sci-fi failure to anticipate network-connected PCs was matched by an equivalently flawed estimation of our future advances in transportation. Most science-fiction writers in the middle of the twentieth century assumed that space travel would become a commonplace civilian activity by the end of the century, while seriously underestimating the impact of the microprocessor, leading to what the sci-fi scholar Gary Westfahl calls "absurd scenes of spaceship pilots frantically manipulating slide rules in order to recalculate their courses." Somehow it was much easier to imagine that human beings would colonize Mars than it was to imagine that they would check the weather and chat with their friends on a PC.

Why were network-connected personal computers so hard to predict? The question is an important one, because the forces that kept our most visionary writers from imagining the digital revolution—and compelled them to wildly overestimate the future of space travel—can tell us a great deal about how predictions fail when we are attempting to forecast the behavior of complex systems. The simplest explanation is what Westfahl calls the "fallacy of extrapolation":

> *This is the assumption that an identified trend will always continue in the same manner, indefinitely into the future. Thus, George Orwell in the 1940s observed steady growth in totalitarian governments and predicted the trend would continue until it engulfed the entire world by the year Nineteen Eighty-Four. . . . Robert A. Heinlein in "Where To?" (1952) was one of many commentators who, noticing that the extent of clothing that society requires people to wear had steadily declined during the last century, confidently predicted the future acceptance of complete public nudity.*

Space travel is the ultimate example of the fallacy of extrapolation at work. From about 1820 to around 1976—a period bookended by the invention of the railroads on one end and the first supersonic flight of the Concorde on the other—the top speed of the human species accelerated dramatically. We went from the blistering 40 mph of the first locomotives—the fastest any human being had ever traveled—to the supersonic speeds of jet airplanes and rockets in just over a century, more than a twentyfold increase in velocity. It seemed only logical that the trend would continue and humans would soon be traveling at 20,000 mph, thus making travel to Mars not much more consequential than a transatlantic flight on a jet airplane. But, of course, that upward curve in top speed hit a series of unanticipated road-blocks, some of which involved the laws of physics, some of which involved declining funding for space programs around the world. In fact, with the decommissioning of the Concorde, the average civilian top speed of travel has actually *declined* over the past two decades. The prediction of colonies on Mars failed because cur-rent trends did not continue to hold in a steady state.

The networked personal computer was a different kind of problem. For roughly a century and a half, transportation speed was more predictable because the problem of designing engines involved a limited and relatively stable number of disciplines. It was thermodynamics and mechanical engineering, and maybe a little chemistry in experimenting with different kinds of propul-sion sources. But the fields that converged to invent the modern digital computer were far more diverse. Computing began in math, but it came to rely on electrical engineering, robotics, and microwave signal processing, not to mention entirely new fields like user interface design. When all of those different fields are raising their game at a regular pace, category-changing break-throughs can arise, precisely the kind of step change that is dif-ficult to predict in advance. The fact that the chips got so cheap can be attributed to both the advances in solid state physics that enabled us to use semiconductors as logic gates and, eventually, to advances in supply chain management that enable a device like the iPhone to be assembled out of components made on another continent.

This is why so many smart people had a blind spot for the

personal computer. To see it coming, you had to understand that the symbolic languages of programming would advance beyond the simple mathematical calculations of early computation; you had to understand that silicon and integrated circuits would replace vacuum tubes; that radio waves could be manipulated to convey binary information, instead of analog waveforms; that the electrons firing at cathode-ray screens could be controlled so precisely that they could form legible alphanumeric characters; that stable networks could form on top of decentralized nodes without any master device controlling the entire system. To make sense of it all, you had to be a mathematician, and a supply chain manager, and an information theorist, and a solid state physicist. For all its achievements, the physical acceleration of the nineteenth and twentieth centuries was all just a variation on a single theme: burn something, and convert the energy released into movement. But the computer was a symphony.

Is the myopia of Tetlock's pundits and the sci-fi authors perhaps just a sign that complex systems like geopolitics and information technology are fundamentally unpredictable because they involve too many variables, distributed across too many different fields? And if that's the case, how can we ever make better long-term decisions? To make successful decisions, you need to have a better-than-chance understanding of where the paths you're choosing between are going to take you. You can't be farsighted if the road ahead is blurry.

Are there fields where we have made meaningful advances in predicting the future behavior of complex systems, not just incremental improvements of the superforecasters? And if so, can we learn something from their success?

THE WATER CURE

A few years after Darwin made his fateful decision to marry, he began experiencing mysterious bouts of vomiting, a condition that would plague him for the rest of his life. Eventually his physicians recommended that he leave London to recuperate. The doctors weren't simply sending him to the country for a little rest and relaxation. They had a much more specific intervention in mind. They were sending him to the water cure.

In taking their advice, Darwin was following the lead of many of his intellectual peers: Alfred Tennyson, Florence Nightingale, Charles Dickens, and George Eliot's companion, George Henry Lewes. Situated near a legendary natural spring in the town of Malvern, the water cure clinic had been founded a decade before by two doctors named James Manby Gully and James Wilson. In modern terms, the Malvern clinic would be categorized at the extreme end of "holistic" health practices, but at the time, it was largely indistinguishable from genuine medicine. Darwin made several visits to Malvern and wrote many letters mulling the scientific validity of the water cure. (As we will see, he had reason to be concerned. The great tragedy of his life unfurled during a trip to Malvern.) The treatments Gully and Wilson devised included dumping a large quantity of freezing-cold water onto their patients and then wrapping them in wet sheets and forcing them to lie still for hours. Gully, in particular, seems to have been receptive to just about every holistic or spiritual treatment one could imagine. In a letter, Darwin mocked his doctor for the "medical" interventions he arranged for his own family: "When his daughter was very ill," he wrote of Gully, "he had a clairvoyant girl to report on internal changes, a mesmerist to put her to sleep, a homeopathist . . . and himself as hydropathist."

The fact that Darwin kept returning to Malvern despite his misgivings suggests that he still believed there was something genuinely therapeutic about the water cure. While it is likely true that the simple act of leaving the polluted chaos of London and drinking uncontaminated water for a few weeks would have had health benefits, the specific treatments employed at the clinic almost certainly had no positive effect on the patients' condition other than perhaps the small bonus of the placebo effect. The fact that the water cure appears to have had no medical value whatsoever did not stop Gully and Wilson from developing a national reputation as miracle healers.

That reputation may have had something to do with the fact that the water cure outperformed many common medical interventions from the period: arsenic, lead, and bloodletting were all still commonly prescribed by the most highly regarded physicians. When you think of some of the engineering and scientific achievements of the period—Darwin's dangerous idea, the railroads—it seems strangely asynchronous that medical expertise would still be lingering in such dark age mysticism. Darwin faced one of the most challenging decisions one can imagine—What treatment should I seek for this debilitating illness?—and his options were fundamentally, Should I let this doctor dump a bucket of ice water on me, or should I opt for the leeches?

That choice seems laughable to us today, but how did it come about in the first place? The Victorians were great overachievers in many fields. Why were they so incompetent with medicine? There is a good argument to be made that, in sum, the medical professions of the Victorian era broke the Hippocratic oath and did more harm than good with their interventions. The average Victorian trying to stay alive in that environment would have done better ignoring all medical advice than paying attention to any of it.

There are many reasons for that strange deficit, but one of them is this: Victorian doctors were incapable of predicting the future in any reliable way, at least in terms of the effects of their treatments. They might have promised you that being doused in ice water or poisoned with arsenic would cure your tuberculosis. But they had no real way of knowing whether their actions had any effect on the disease. Every medical prophecy was based on anecdote, intuition, and hearsay. And that lack of foresight was only partly due to the fact that Victorian doctors didn't have access to the medical tools that we now take for granted: X-ray machines, fMRI scanners, electron microscopes. They also lacked a *conceptual* tool: randomized controlled trials.

In 1948, the *British Medical Journal* published a paper called "Streptomycin treatment of pulmonary tuberculosis"—an analysis of the effects of a new antibiotic in treating victims of tuberculosis, coauthored by many researchers but led by the British statistician and epidemiologist Austin Bradford Hill. Streptomycin was, in fact, a step forward in treating the disease, but what made Hill's research so revolutionary was not the content of the study but rather its form. "Streptomycin treatment of pulmonary tuberculosis" is widely considered to be the first randomized controlled trial in the history of medical research.

There are inventions that shape how we manipulate matter in the world. And then there are inventions that shape how we manipulate data, new methods that let us see patterns in that data that we couldn't have seen before. The tuberculosis experiment, like all randomized controlled trials, relied on a kind of crowd wisdom. It wasn't enough to just give the antibiotic to one or two patients and report whether they lived or died. Hill's streptomycin study involved more than a hundred subjects, randomly divided into two groups, one given the antibiotic and one given a placebo.

Once you put those elements together—a large enough sample size, and a randomly selected control group—something extraordinary happened: you had a tool for separating genuine medical interventions from quackery. You could make a prediction about future events—in this case, you could predict the outcome of prescribing streptomycin to a patient suffering from pulmonary tuberculosis. Your forecast wasn't always 100 percent accurate, of course, but for the first time doctors could map out chains of cause and effect with genuine rigor, even if they didn't understand all the underlying forces that made those causal chains a reality. If someone proposed that the water cure offered a better treatment for tuberculosis, you could test the hypothesis empirically. Almost immediately, the randomized controlled trial began changing the course of medical history. Just a few years after the tuberculosis trial, Hill went on to do a landmark RCT analyzing the health effects of cigarette smoking, arguably the first methodologically sound study to prove that tobacco smoke was harmful to our health.

The interesting thing about the RCT is how late it arrived on the stage of scientific progress. The germ theory didn't become an established idea until we had microscopes powerful enough to see bacteria and viruses. Freud famously gave up his study of the physiological works of the brain because he didn't have access to scanning tools like fMRI machines. But the idea of a randomized controlled experiment wasn't impeded by some not-yet-invented tool. You could have easily conducted one in 1748. (In fact, the British ship doctor James Lind almost stumbled upon the methodology right around then while investigating the cause of scurvy, but his technique never caught on, and Lind himself seems to have not fully believed the results of his experiment.)

You could see Darwin straining toward the structure of the RCT in his interactions with Gully and the water cure. He took to maintaining a ledger of sorts that tracked the date and time of each treatment he applied, his physical state before the intervention, and his subsequent state the night after. (One gets the sense that Darwin would have been an avid Fitbit user.) This early rendition of what we would now call the "quantified self" had an earnest scientific question at its core: Darwin was looking for patterns in the data that could help him decide whether Gully was a quack or a visionary. He was running a sequential experiment on his own body. The architecture of the experiment was lacking a few foundational elements: you can't run an RCT on a single subject, and you need some kind of "control" to measure the effects of the intervention. However meticulous Darwin was in recording his water cure experiment, by definition he couldn't give *himself* a placebo.

In the decades that followed, a small but growing chorus of voices began to argue that a new statistical method might be possible in evaluating the efficacy of different medical interventions, but it was not at all clear how revolutionary the technique was going to be. As late as 1923, *The Lancet* asked the question, "Is the application of the numerical method to the subject-matter of medicine a trivial and time-wasting ingenuity as some hold, or is it an important stage in the development of our art, as others proclaim it?" Reading the lines now, they seem remarkably naive. ("Will this new alphabetic writing technology really make a difference, or will it just turn out to be a fad? Experts disagree.") But we now know, beyond a shadow of a doubt, that the randomized controlled experiment was not just "an important stage in the development of our art," as *The Lancet* put it. It was, in fact, the breakthrough that turned medicine from an art into a science. For the first time, a patient confronting a bewildering choice about how to treat a disease or ailment could learn from the experiences of hundreds or thousands of other people who had faced a similar challenge. The RCT gave human beings a new superpower, not unlike the unimaginably fast calculations of the digital computer or the breathtaking propulsion of the jet engine. In this one area of complex decision-making—What treatment should I pursue to rid myself of this illness?—we can now predict the future with an acuity that would have been unimaginable just four generations ago.

THE FIRST FORECAST

The ironclad ocean steamer *Royal Charter*, its cargo hulls weighed down with bounty from the Australian gold rush, had almost reached the end of its 14,000-mile journey from Melbourne to Liverpool when the winds began to rise late in the afternoon of October 25, 1859. Legend has it that the captain, Thomas Taylor, overruled a suggestion that they take harbor after the barometers began to drop precipitously. It seemed preposterous not to simply outrun the storm with Liverpool so close. Within hours, though, the storm exploded into one of the most powerful ever recorded in the Irish Sea. Quickly surrendering his Liverpool plan, the captain lowered the sails and anchored near the coast, but the winds and rough sea soon overpowered the ship. Battered by hurricane-level gales, the *Royal Charter* smashed against the rocks near the Welsh town of Anglesey, only seventy miles from Liverpool. The ship broke into three pieces and sank. Around 450 passengers and crew perished, many of them killed violently on the rocky shores.

The *Royal Charter* storm, as it came to be called, ultimately claimed almost a thousand lives and destroyed hundreds of ships along the coasts of England, Scotland, and Wales. In the weeks that followed the storm, Robert FitzRoy—Darwin's captain from the voyage of the *Beagle*—read the reports with growing outrage from his office in London. FitzRoy had traded in his career as a captain for a desk job running the Meteorological Department of the Board of Trade (now called, colloquially, the Met Office), which he had founded in 1854.

Today, the Met Office is the government agency responsible for weather forecasting in the United Kingdom, the equivalent of the National Weather Service in the United States, but the initial purview of the office had nothing to do with predicting *future* weather events. Instead, FitzRoy had established the department to calculate faster shipping routes by studying wind patterns around the globe. The science of the Met Office wasn't trying to determine what the weather was going to do tomorrow. It simply wanted to know what the weather *generally* did. Predicting the weather belonged entirely to the world of folk wisdom and sham almanacs. When a member of Parliament suggested in 1854 that it might be scientifically possible to predict London's weather twenty-four hours in advance, he was greeted with howls of laughter. But FitzRoy and a few other visionaries had begun to imagine turning the charade of weather prognostication into something resembling a science. FitzRoy was assisted by three important developments, all of which had come into place in the preceding decade: a crude but functional understanding of the connection between storm winds and troughs of low pressure, increasingly accurate barometers that could measure changes in atmospheric pressure, and a network of telegraphs that could transmit those readings back to the Met Office headquarters in London.

Galvanized by the disaster of the Royal Charter storm, FitzRoy established a network of fourteen stations in towns on the English coast, recording weather data and transmitting to headquarters for analysis. Working with a small team in the Met Office, transcribing the data by hand, FitzRoy created the first generation of meteorological charts, offering maritime travelers the advance warning that the lost souls of the *Royal Charter* had lacked.

Initially the Met Office used the data exclusively to warn ships of upcoming storms, but it quickly became apparent that they were assembling predictions that would be of interest for civilian life on land as well. FitzRoy coined a new term for these predictions to differentiate them from the quack soothsaying that had been standard up until that point. He called his weather reports "forecasts." "Prophecies and predictions they are not," he explained. "The term forecast is strictly applicable to such an opinion as is the result of scientific combination and calculation."

The first scientifically grounded forecast appeared in the *Times* (London) on August 1, 1861, predicting a temperature in London of 62°F, clear skies, and a southwesterly wind. The forecast proved to be accurate—the temperature peaked at 61°F that day—and before long, weather forecasts became a staple of most newspapers, even if they were rarely as accurate as FitzRoy's initial prediction.

Despite the telegraph network and the barometers—and FitzRoy's bravado about "scientific combination and calculation"—the predictive powers of meteorology in the nineteenth century were still very limited. FitzRoy published a tome explaining his theories of weather formation in 1862, most of which have not stood the test of time. A review of the Met Office forecasting technique—allegedly conducted by the brilliant statistician Francis Galton—found that "no notes or calculations are made. The operation takes about half an hour and is conducted mentally." (Stung by the critiques, and by his implicit role in supporting what he considered the sacrilegious theory of evolution, FitzRoy committed suicide in 1865.) Weather forecasters couldn't build real-time models of the atmosphere, so instead they relied on a kind of historical pattern recognition. They created charts that documented data received from all the observational stations, mapping the reported temperature, pressure, humidity, wind, and precipitation. Those charts were then stored as a historical record of past configurations. When a new configuration emerged, the forecasters would consult earlier charts that resembled the current pattern and use that as a guide for predicting the next day's weather. If there was a low pressure system and cool southern winds off the coast of Wales, with a warm high over

Surrey, the forecasters would go back and find a comparable day from the past, and figure out what the weather did over the next few days in that previous instance. It was more of an educated guess than a proper forecast, and its predictive powers went steadily downhill outside the twenty-four-hour range, but it was a meaningful leap forward from the tea-leaf reading that had characterized all weather predictions before that point.

As the science of fluid dynamics evolved over the first decades of the twentieth century, it became possible to imagine actually modeling the internal behavior of weather systems, and not just looking at surface resemblances between different configurations. Lewis Fry Richardson proposed a "Weather Prediction by Numerical Process" in a short, equation-heavy book by the same title in 1923, right around the time *The Lancet* was pondering the merits of a statistical approach to medicine. The problem with Richardson's proposal—which he himself was all too aware of—lay in the complexity of the calculations: you couldn't crunch the numbers within the window of the prediction itself. You might be able to build a model that could predict the weather twenty-four hours from now, but it would take you *thirty-six* hours to actually run the calculations. Richardson sensed that mechanical devices might be invented that would accelerate the process, but his tone was not altogether hopeful: "Perhaps some day in the dim future it will be possible to advance the computations faster than the weather advances and at a cost less than the saving to mankind due to the information gained. But that is a dream."

Those mechanical devices did arrive, of course, and by the 1970s, national weather bureaus were modeling atmospheric systems with computers, generating forecasts in hours, not days. Today they are still occasionally prone to embarrassing (and sometimes deadly) blind spots. The behavior of hyperlocal weather systems—like tornadoes—are still difficult to map in advance, but it is very rare indeed that a tornado touches ground on a day without a regional warning twenty-four hours in advance. Daily forecasts are now remarkably accurate on an hour-by-hour basis. But the real improvement has been with the long-term forecast. Ten-day forecasts were virtually useless just a generation ago. Looking beyond the window of the next forty-eight hours put you back in *Farmers' Almanac* territory. Today, ten-day forecasts far outperform chance, particularly in winter months when the weather systems are larger and thus easier to model. This improvement is not simply a matter of doing more calculations per second. The new weather models are so much more accurate than their predecessors because they rely on an entirely new technique, what is conventionally called ensemble forecasting. Instead of measuring the initial conditions of the current weather and predicting a future sequence of weather events based on a "numerical process" like the one Lewis Fry Richardson proposed, ensemble forecasts create hundreds or thousands of different forecasts, and in each separate simulation the computer alters the initial conditions slightly—lowering the pressure by a few notches here, raising the temperature a few degrees there. If ninety out of a hundred simulations show the hurricane picking up speed and shifting to the northeast, then the meteorologists issue a high-probability forecast that the hurricane is going to pick up speed and shift to the northeast. If only 50 percent of the simulations suggest that pattern, then they issue a forecast with less certainty.

People still make casual jokes about how incompetent meteorologists are, but in fact, thanks to the meta-technique of ensemble forecasting, they have been getting steadily more accurate over the past few decades. A chaotic system like weather may never be fully predictable beyond a few weeks, given the number of variables and the baroque chains of influence that connect them. But our forecasting skills have expanded at a remarkable rate over the past few decades. Weather forecasts are so ubiquitous that we rarely stop to think about them, but the fact is, in this one realm, we can now predict the future with an accuracy that would have astounded our grandparents. In a literal sense, those ensemble simulations, like the randomized controlled experiments of medical research, gave us a new power of clairvoyance. Our ability to predict is no longer just dependent on the what-if scenarios of the default network. We have strategies and technologies that extend our view into the future. The question is, can we apply those tools to other kinds of decisions?

SIMULATIONS

When we make hard choices, we are implicitly making predictions about the course of future events. When we decide to build a park on the outskirts of a growing city, we are predicting that the park will attract regular visitors; that the city itself will expand to envelop the park over the coming years; that replacing the open space with commercial development would, in the long run, prove to be a net negative for the city as greenery becomes increasingly scarce. None of those outcomes are predetermined. They are all predictions, with a meaningful margin of error. So when we see other ways of predicting—medical, say, or meteorological—achieve a positive step-change in accuracy, we should pay attention. Think about Tetlock's foxes and hedge-hogs. The fact that the social forecasters were better served by having a diverse set of interests—and an openness to experience—suggests a lesson that could be directly applied to the domain of personal choices. In Tetlock's study, the narrowband approach didn't just make you indistinguishable from the dart-throwing chimp; it made you *worse*. That alone should give us one valuable lesson: In the hard choice, single-minded focus is overrated.

Think of these three forecasts—the medical predictions of randomized controlled trials, the meteorological predictions of the weather forecasts, and the social predictions of the futur-ists and the pundits—as three patients, suffering from a chronic form of myopia that keeps them from accurately envisioning fu-ture events. The first two patients suffered along with the third for all of human history, until a handful of new ideas converged in the late nineteenth and early twentieth centuries that enabled them to improve their clairvoyant powers in empirically verifiable ways. The time scales were different: the RCTs let us see years, even decades, into the future; the weather forecasts let us see a week. They both hit some kind of threshold point that turned the noise of false prophecy into meaningful signal, but the social forecasters experienced no equivalent step-change. Why?

For all their differences, the RCTs and the weather forecasts share one defining characteristic. They both find wisdom about the question they are wrestling with—Is this medicine going to help treat my illness? Will the hurricane cross over land on Tuesday?—through multiple *simulations*. In an RCT, those simulations take the form of the hundreds or thousands of other patients with a similar medical condition administered a drug or a placebo. In a weather forecast, the simulations are the hundreds or thousands of atmospheric models generated with an ensemble forecast, each featuring slight variations in the initial conditions. Those patients in the drug trial are not exact replicas of you and your own individual condition, in all its complexity, but they are close enough, and because there are so many of them, the aggregate patterns in the data can tell you something useful about the long-term effects of the drug you are considering taking.

Societal predictions, on the other hand, do not usually have the luxury of consulting alternate realities where the forecast in question—Will the Soviet Union survive the 1990s?—is simulated hundreds of times. This is key to understanding why our medical and meteorological forecasts have gotten so much more accurate, while our societal forecasts have remained so murky. It's not that social or technological change is more *complicated* as a system—the Earth's atmosphere is the very definition of a complex system, after all—it's that we don't usually have access to simulations when we talk about future changes to geopolitics or technological inventions.

Ensemble simulations are so powerful, in fact, that you don't necessarily need to have a complete understanding of how the system works to make useful predictions about its future behavior. When Austin Bradford Hill and his team were experimenting with streptomycin in the late 1940s, they didn't understand the cell biology that explained *why* the antibiotic combated tuberculosis in the way modern medicine now does. But the RCT enabled them to develop the treatment regimen anyway, because the data they generated by giving the drug (and a placebo) to hundreds of patients allowed them to see a pattern that was not necessarily visible from giving the drug to just a single patient.

Simulations make us better decision-makers, because simulations make us better at predicting future events, even when the system we are trying to model contains thousands or millions of variables. But, of course, it's much harder to explore small-group decisions through randomized controlled trials or ensemble forecasting. We would get better at predicting the impact pathways of our professional choices if we could run alternate versions of our experience in parallel, and experiment with different choices and outcomes. Rewind the tape and try your career again—only this time you and your partners decide to open a restaurant in a different neighborhood or switch from a restaurant to a boutique. How does that one choice change the future course of your life? Darwin predicted that getting married would reduce his supply of "conversation of clever men at clubs," but if he'd been able to run multiple simulations of his life—some where he marries Emma, and some where he remains a bachelor—he would have had a better sense of whether that sacrifice actually turned out to be a real one. Simulations make us better at predicting, and successful predictions make us better decision-makers. How, then, can we simulate the personal or collective choices that matter most in our lives?

THE GAME

On the night of April 7, 2011, two stealth Black Hawk helicopters approached a three-story compound, ringed by concrete walls and barbed wire. In the cover of darkness, one Black Hawk hovered over the roof while a SEAL Team 6 unit descended via rope to the roof of the structure. Another chopper deposited a different unit in the courtyard. Minutes later, the units ascended back into the choppers and disappeared into the night.

No guns were fired over the course of this operation, and no terrorist masterminds were captured, because the compound in question did not lie on the outskirts of Abbottabad but rather on the grounds of Fort Bragg, North Carolina. As President Obama contemplated his four options for attacking the Pakistan compound, the Special Ops team, led by General William McRaven, had begun simulating the proposed helicopter raid. The tabletop scale model of the compound had been replaced by a real-life structure built to the exact dimensions of the Abbottabad building and grounds. If there was something in the structure of the compound that made a Special Ops raid unmanageable, McRaven wanted to discover it before Obama decided on the ultimate plan of attack.

And yet, even with the architectural details of the re-created compound, the simulation at Fort Bragg couldn't re-create one critical element of the actual raid: the hot, high-altitude climate of northeastern Pakistan. And so several weeks later, the same team gathered at a base in Nevada, four thousand feet above sea level—almost the exact elevation of the compound. For this exercise, McRaven did not bother to build an entire simulated structure to represent the compound. They just stacked some Conex shipping containers and surrounded them with chain-link fences roughly corresponding to the location of the concrete walls. This simulation was more focused on the helicopters and their performance at that altitude. "On the real mission the helicopters would have to fly ninety minutes before arriving over Abbottabad," Mark Bowden writes. "They would be flying very low and very fast to avoid Pakistani radar. Mission planners had to test precisely what the choppers could do at that altitude and in the anticipated air temperatures. How much of a load could the choppers carry and still perform? Originally they had thought they might be able to make it there and back without refueling, but the margins were too close. The choppers would have been coming back on fumes. So the refueling area was necessary."

We expect our military forces to rehearse a dangerous mission before embarking on it. But the simulated raids in North Carolina and Nevada were staged *before* Obama actually made the decision to use the Black Hawks to attack the compound. The Special Ops forces weren't simply practicing for an attack; they were simulating the attack in order to better understand what might go wrong once the Black Hawks entered Pakistani airspace. The simulations were a crucial part of the decision process itself. What they were looking for, ultimately, was some unanticipated consequence of staging the raid in that particular situation. The notorious attempt to rescue the Iranian hostages in 1980 had failed in part because the helicopters encountered a severe dust storm called a haboob—common in the Middle East—that crippled one of the helicopters and ultimately forced the mission to be aborted. If McRaven was going to remain an advocate for the SEAL Team 6 option, he wanted to explore all the potential ways the mission could go wrong.

"One thing a person cannot do, no matter how rigorous his analysis or heroic his imagination," the Nobel laureate Thomas Schelling once observed, "is to draw up a list of things that would never occur to him." And yet hard choices usually require us to make those kinds of imaginative leaps: to discover new possibilities that had not been visible to us when we first started wrestling with the decision; to find our way, somehow, to the unknown unknowns lurking outside our field of vision. A brilliant economist and foreign policy analyst, Schelling had a capacity for "rigorous analysis" rivaled by few. But in his years working with the RAND Corporation in the late 1950s and 1960s, he became an advocate for a less rigorous way of thinking around our blind spots: playing games.

The war games designed by Schelling and his RAND colleague Herman Kahn have been well documented by historians and other chroniclers of the period. They led to everything from the controversial theory of Mutually Assured Destruction that governed so much of Cold War military strategy to the creation of the "red phone" hotline between Washington and Moscow to the character of Dr. Strangelove in Stanley Kubrick's classic film. But the tradition of war-gaming has much older roots. In the first decades of the nineteenth century, a father-and-son team of Prussian military officers created a dice-based game called Kriegsspiel (literally "war game" in German) that simulated military combat. The game resembled a much more complex version of modern games like Risk. Players placed pawns that represented different military units on a map, and the game could accommodate up to ten players working on different teams with a hierarchical command system inside each team. Kriegsspiel even had game mechanisms to account for communications breakdowns between commanders and troops in the field, simulating the "fog of war." Like the modern-day game Battleship, Kriegsspiel was played on two separate boards, so each side had incomplete knowledge of the other's actions. A "gamemaster"—an early precedent of the Dungeon Masters that emerged with fantasy games in the 1970s—shuffled back and forth between the two boards, overseeing the play.

Kriegsspiel became an essential part of officer training in the Prussian military. Translated versions of the game made their way into other nations' armed forces after the string of military victories under Bismarck's command suggested that the game was giving the Prussians a tactical advantage in battle. It may have played a role in the ultimately disastrous military actions of World War I. The Germans had used Kriegsspiel to simulate invading Holland and Belgium before taking aim at the French. "The game determined that Germany would triumph against France," the conceptual artist and philosopher Jonathon Keats writes, "as long as ammunition could be rapidly replenished. For this purpose, Germany built the world's first motorized supply battalions, deployed in 1914. And the plan might have worked brilliantly, if the only players had been the German and French armies." Instead, the game failed to anticipate the extent to which Belgian saboteurs would undermine their own railway system (and thus the German supply chain), and it had no mechanism for simulating the diplomacy that would eventually bring the United States into the conflict.

The Naval War College in the United States had conducted paper-based war games since its founding in 1884, but in the decade after World War I, the navy took war-gaming to new heights by staging a series of mock conflicts using actual planes and warships (though without bombs and bullets). The exercises—formally designated as "Fleet Problems" followed by a Roman numeral—explored everything from a defense of the Panama Canal to the growing threat of submarine attacks. Fleet Problem

XIII, conducted in 1932 over a vast stretch of ocean—from Hawaii to San Diego all the way north to the Puget Sound—simulated an aerial attack on US military bases from the Pacific. The exercise made it clear that US forces were vulnerable to a "determined aggressor" to the country's west, and suggested that six to eight carrier battle groups would be required to mount a proper defense. The advice was ignored, in large part because of the budgetary constraints of the Great Depression. But the prediction would turn out to be tragically accurate on December 7, 1941. If the US military had successfully applied the lesson of Fleet Problem XIII, it is entirely possible that the Japanese attack on Pearl Harbor would have failed—or would have never been attempted in the first place.

Not all war games were perfect crystal balls. But as a mental exercise, they functioned in much the same way as randomized controlled trials or ensemble weather forecasts. They created a platform where decisions could be rehearsed multiple times, using different strategies with each round. The collaborative nature of game play—even if you were playing a zero-sum, competitive game—meant that new possibilities and configurations could become visible to you thanks to unexpected moves that your opponent put on the table. War games began with a map—one of the key innovations that made Kriegsspiel different from metaphoric military games like chess is that it used an actual topographic map of the field of battle—but the real revelation of the game arose from how it forced you to *explore* that map, to simulate all the different ways the opposing armies might do battle in that space. In Schelling's language, you can't draw up a list of things that will never occur to you. But you can *play* your way into that kind of list. If Kriegsspiel had been invented—and popularized—a century earlier, it's not hard to imagine Washington successfully anticipating the British attack through Jamaica Pass. The simulations of the war game might well have made up for the local intelligence he lost when Nathanael Greene fell ill.

Gameplay as a guide to complex decision-making has historically been dominated by military applications, but it has much broader potential as a tool. After participating in some RAND-sponsored war games simulating the conflict in East Asia, then attorney general Robert Kennedy inquired if a comparable game could be developed to help understand the Kennedy administration's options in promoting civil rights gains in the American South. (The project, sadly, was dropped after his brother's assassination.) Shortly thereafter, Buckminster Fuller proposed the development of a kind of mirror-image version of the Pentagon war games: a "world peace game" that anticipated subsequent video games like *Civilization* or *SimCity*. The game was designed to be played on a special map that could track everything from ocean currents to trade routes. The rules were explicitly non–zero-sum in nature, designed to encourage collaboration, not conflict. "The objective of the game would be to explore for ways to make it possible for anybody and everybody in the human family to enjoy the total earth without any human interfering with any other human and without any human gaining advantage at the expense of another," Fuller wrote. "To win the World Game everybody must be made physically successful. Everybody must win." Fuller saw the game as a kind of alternative to the indirect decision-making mechanisms of the democratic process. Instead of electing leaders to make decisions, ordinary people would simulate through gameplay the challenges they faced. "Winning" strategies—in other words, strategies that led to positive outcomes for all—would then be translated into real-life programs.

There does seem to be genuine merit in using games to trigger new ideas and explore the possibility space of a particularly challenging decision. It seems harder to imagine applying the gameplay approach to one's personal decisions—designing a game, for instance, to rehearse that potential move to the suburbs. But almost every decision can be productively rehearsed with another, even more ancient form of escapism: storytelling.

SCENARIO PLANS

In the mid-1970s, the environmental activist and occasional entrepreneur Paul Hawken was working with a nonprofit in Palo Alto that taught "intensive gardening" techniques to developing countries as a way of combating nutritional and vitamin A deficiencies. Hawken had lived in the UK for a while and had seen how English gardeners tended to use higher quality tools than most Americans did. "Wealthy Americans were buying cheap tools," Hawken would later recall, "and poor people there were buying what we call expensive tools, but which were cheaper over the life of the tool." Hawken figured the tools might be helpful for the nonprofit's initiatives, so he ordered an entire container of them from a British company called Bulldog Tools, but by the time they arrived, the head of the nonprofit had had a change of heart and Hawken found himself in possession of a container full of upscale garden tools with no obvious way to get rid of them. Ultimately, he partnered with a friend named Dave Smith to create a company called Fundamental Tools to sell the British imports to Bay Area gardeners. Before long, they changed the name to Smith and Hawken, because "it sounded so English, old, and solid."

As the company began to grow, they started to contemplate whether they could break out to a larger audience. The challenge was that the tools were significantly more expensive—as much as three times the cost—than what American consumers were accustomed to paying. Would there be a large enough market of people willing to shell out thirty dollars for a shovel when they'd spent their entire gardening life paying only ten? One of the investors they approached during the period was a fellow Bay Area resident named Peter Schwartz, who would later go on to write a number of influential books and cofound organizations like the Global Business Network and the Long Now Foundation. Schwartz was an experienced practitioner of a technique known as scenario planning, a decision-making tool that had been developed at Royal Dutch Shell in the late sixties by Pierre Wack and Ted Newland. (Schwartz would go on to replace Wack at Shell after Wack retired in the mid-eighties.) Scenario planning is a narrative art, first and foremost. It homes in on the uncertainties that inevitably haunt a complex decision and forces the participants to imagine multiple versions of how that uncertain future might actually play out. Wack had famously used scenario planning at Shell to anticipate the oil crisis of the mid-seventies. Schwartz would later use the same technique to evaluate the prospects for Smith and Hawken's garden tool business. Building those scenarios required full-spectrum mapping. He analyzed urban-versus-suburban migration patterns that might affect the market size for gardeners; he looked at an emerging trend in

US consumer behavior where there appeared to be a new appetite for more expensive European brands, like BMW or Bang & Olufsen; he contemplated macroeconomic possibilities; and he surveyed then-fringe movements like organic farming and environmental activism. But he combined all that research into three distinct stories, imagining three distinct futures: a high-growth model, a depression model, and what he called the transformative model: "a shift in values that would amount to a profound transformation of Western culture. Ideas had begun to circulate about living more simply and environmentally benignly, about holistic medicine and natural foods, about pursuing inner growth rather than material possessions, and about striving for some kind of planetary consciousness." The three-part structure turns out to be a common refrain in scenario planning: you build one model where things get better, one where they get worse, and one where they get weird.

Schwartz ultimately decided that the company's future was promising, no matter which scenario came to pass, and he made a small investment in the company, which was soon selling millions of dollars of fancy trowels to American gardeners. Hawken and Schwartz began thinking about the scenario-planning technique as a tool for making broader social decisions: environmental stewardship, tax and wealth distribution policies, trade agreements. With a third author named Jay Ogilvy, they published a book in the early 1980s called *Seven Tomorrows* that sketched out seven distinct scenarios for the next two decades. In the introduction, they explained their approach: "Among the many methods for probing the future—from elaborate computer models to simple extrapolations of history—we chose the scenario

method because it allows for the inclusion of realism and imagination, comprehensiveness and uncertainty, and, most of all, because the scenario method permits a genuine plurality of options."
What differentiated the scenario-planning approach from most flavors of futurism was its unwillingness to fixate on a single forecast. By forcing themselves to imagine alternatives, scenario planners avoided the trap of Tetlock's hedgehogs, settled in their one big idea. Like Schelling's war games, the scenario plan was a tool to help you think of something you would never otherwise think of.

In corporate culture, scenario planning built its reputation on the mythologies of these famously accurate forecasts, like Pierre Wack "calling" the oil crisis three years before OPEC suddenly jacked up its prices. But the emphasis on successful prophecies misses the point. Most scenarios end up failing to predict future outcomes, but the very act of trying to imagine alternatives to the conventional view helps you perceive your options more clearly. Scenario planning is genuinely not intended to be consulted for an *accurate* forecast of future events. Instead, it primes you to resist the "fallacy of extrapolation." Wack described this property in terms of the defining chaos of the modern business environment, but the principle applies to the chaos of one's private life as well:

> [T]he way to solve this problem is not to look for better forecasts by perfecting techniques or hiring more or better forecasters. Too many forces work against the possibility of getting the right forecast. The future is no longer stable; it has become a moving target. No single "right" projection can be deduced

from past behavior. The better approach, I believe, is to accept uncertainty, try to understand it, and make it part of our reasoning. Uncertainty today is not just an occasional, temporary deviation from a reasonable predictability; it is a basic structural feature of the business environment.

Every decision relies on predictions with varying degrees of certainty. If you are contemplating a move to a suburban house that abuts a public park with extensive hiking trails, you can predict with some certainty that access to natural space will be part of the house's appeal if you do choose to buy it. If you're contemplating a fixed-rate thirty-year mortgage, you can project out the monthly payments you'll be required to pay with even more conviction. If you know something about the overall reputation of the neighborhood school, you can be reasonably confident that those general academic standards will persist over the coming years, though it is harder to know exactly how your children will adapt to the new school. A scenario-based exploration of a potential move to the suburbs would take the elements that are most uncertain, and imagine different outcomes for each of them. It is, at heart, a kind of informed storytelling, and of course storytelling is something we instinctively do anytime we are contemplating a big decision. If we're leaning toward life in the suburbs, we tell a story of family hikes through the trails behind our house, and better public schools, and a garden that we can tend with high-priced imported tools. The difference with the storytelling of scenario planning is twofold: first, we rarely take the time to do a full-spectrum analysis of all the forces that shape that story; and second, we rarely bother to construct *multiple* stories. How does the story unfold if the kids don't like their classmates, or if one part of the family loves the new lifestyle but the other is homesick for the vitality and old friends of city life?

As Wack suggests, that uncertainty can't simply be analyzed out of existence. It is, on some fundamental level, an irreducible property of complex systems. What scenario planning—and simulations in general—offer us is a way of rehearsing for that uncertainty. That doesn't always give you a definite path, but it does prepare you for the many ways that the future might unexpectedly veer from its current trajectory. "A sustained scenario practice can make leaders comfortable with the ambiguity of an open future," Wack writes. "It can counter hubris, expose assumptions that would otherwise remain implicit, contribute to shared and systemic sense-making, and foster quick adaptation in times of crisis."

Much of the decision process that led up to the bin Laden operation had focused on simulating the minute-by-minute execution of the raid itself: Would the helicopters need refueling? Could the SEAL Team 6 unit be successfully deployed on the roof of the compound? In the months and years that followed the raid, most of the coverage focused on those perilous minutes in Pakistan, and the courage and quick thinking of the men who brought bin Laden to justice. But behind the scenes, the Obama administration was not just running simulations of the raid itself. They were also exploring long-term scenarios—the downstream effects of each option on the table. In this, Obama and his team were also learning from the mistakes of the Bush administration, which had notoriously failed to scenario-plan for a long and combative occupation of Iraq, preferring instead to work under Dick

Cheney's assumption that we would be "greeted as liberators" by the Iraqi population.

For Obama and his advisors, one of the key scenarios involved the crucial question of what to do with bin Laden himself, assuming he was discovered on the premises. Should the Special Ops forces try to capture him alive? If so, what would the plan be from there? The president believed there was an opportunity to undo many of the questionable decisions his predecessor had made, with the detention programs at Guantánamo and other extradition sites, by putting bin Laden on trial in a public court in the United States. "My belief was if we had captured him," Obama later explained, "that I would be in a pretty strong position, politically, here, to argue that displaying due process and rule of law would be our best weapon against al-Qaeda, in preventing him from appearing as a martyr." That scenario, of course, would rule out the drone strike and the B-2 bombing, both of which were operations with a single objective: killing Osama bin Laden. The troubling long-term consequences of those two operations were of a different nature: if you wiped the compound off the map with a bomb strike, there would be no direct evidence that bin Laden had, in fact, been killed. Even if the United States intercepted internal conversations within al-Qaeda suggesting their leader had died, rumors and conspiracy theories about his continued existence might proliferate over the years. To make the right choice, it wasn't sufficient to simulate the raid or the bombing strike on the scale of minutes and hours, because the consequences of those actions would inevitably reverberate for years. They had to imagine a much longer narrative. The present tense of the attack on the compound was shadowed by its possible futures.

PREMORTEMS AND RED TEAMS

So much of scenario planning is ultimately a narrative art. You take the unpredictable haze of future events and turn it into some coherent picture: the market for high-end gardening tools will expand as materialism takes over the culture; the Pakistanis will kick us out of their airspace after they discover our betrayal. The problem, of course, is that storytellers suffer from confirmation bias and overconfidence just like the rest of us. Our brains naturally project outcomes that conform to the way we think the world works. To avoid those pitfalls, you need to trick your mind into entertaining alternative narratives, plot lines that might undermine your assumptions, not confirm them.

In his own practice advising decision-makers, Gary Klein—the originator of the famous fire-in-the-basement case study—has developed a compelling variation on the scenario-planning model, one that requires much less research and deliberation. He calls it a "premortem." As the name suggests, the approach is a twist on the medical procedure of postmortem analysis. In a postmortem, the subject is dead, and the coroner's job is to figure out the cause of death. In a premortem, the sequence is reversed: the coroner is told to imagine that the subject is *going to die*, and asked to imagine the causes that will be responsible for that future death. "Our exercise," Klein explains, "is to ask planners to imagine that it is months into the future and that their plan has been carried out. And it has failed. That is all they know; they have to explain why they think it failed."

Klein's approach draws on some intriguing psychological research that found that people come up with richer and subtler explanations when they are given a potential future event and asked to explain the event as if it has actually happened. In other words, if you simply ask people what's going to happen—and why—their explanatory models are less nuanced and imaginative than if you tell people that X is definitely going to happen and ask them to explain why. In Klein's experience, the premortem has proven to be a much more effective way to tease out the potential flaws in a decision. A whole range of cognitive habits—from the fallacy of extrapolation to overconfidence to confirmation bias—tends to blind us to the potential pitfalls of a decision once we have committed to it. It isn't enough to simply ask yourself, "Are there any flaws here in this plan that I'm missing?" By forcing yourself to imagine scenarios where the decision turned out to be a disastrous one, you can think your way around those blind spots and that false sense of confidence.

As in the mapping stage, the predictions of scenario planning work best when they draw on diverse forms of expertise and values. But there are some inevitable limits on the kind of outsider viewpoints you can incorporate into these deliberative sessions. No doubt the internal discussions leading up to the bin Laden raid would have been well served by including an actual Pakistani official in the decision process. His or her imagined narrative might have been quite different from the one being spun by the analysts at the CIA. As you contemplate a new product launch, it might theoretically be helpful to have a product manager from your direct competitor help scenario-plan the next five years of market evolution, but in practice, you're not going to be able to get him or her in the room with you.

But those outside perspectives can themselves be simulated. The military has a long history of deploying what are conventionally called red teams: a kind of systematic version of devil's advocacy where a group inside the organization is assigned the role of emulating an enemy's behavior. Red-teaming dates back to the original war games like Fleet Problem XIII, but it has taken on new life in the military since a Defense Science Board Task Force report in 2003 recommended that the practice be more widely utilized in the wake of the 9/11 attacks. You can think of a red team as a kind of hybrid of war games and scenario plans: You sketch out a few decision paths with imagined outcomes and invite some of your colleagues to put themselves in the shoes of your enemies or your competitors in the market and dream up imagined responses.

Red teams were an integral part of the hunt for bin Laden. Officials deliberately invoked them as a way to ward off the blind spots and confirmation biases that undermined decisions like the Iraq WMD investigation. Mike Leiter, head of the National Counterterrorism Center, had, in fact, written much of the official report on the WMD fiasco and its root causes, and so was particularly eager not to repeat the same mistakes. In late April, even as SEAL Team 6 was rehearsing the Abbottabad raid in the Nevada desert, Leiter commissioned a red team exercise to explore alternative narratives that could explain the mysterious compound *without* bin Laden actually living there. At one point, Leiter told John Brennan, "You don't want to have a WMD commission come back and say, 'You didn't red-team this one.' I wrote that chapter, John."

The red team Leiter assembled included two new analysts who had not been involved in the investigation at all, to give the project fresh eyes. He gave them forty-eight hours to come up with alternative interpretations that could fit the facts on the ground.

They came up with three scenarios: bin Laden had been in the house, but was no longer living there; it was an active al-Qaeda safe house, but it was occupied by a different al-Qaeda leader; or it belonged to a criminal, unconnected to terrorism, for whom al-Kuwaiti now worked. At the end of the exercise, the team was asked to rate the odds of each scenario, including the fourth scenario that bin Laden was, in fact, in the building. The average of the red team's ratings had it at less than fifty-fifty odds that bin Laden was there—but they also concluded the bin Laden scenario was more likely than any of the other individual scenarios.

Of course, with military exercises, red teams can involve more active simulations than simply sitting around in a conference room dreaming up stories. McRaven developed elaborate red teams to simulate possible responses both from the residents of the compound and from the Pakistani military in the event that they detected the helicopters during their incursion into Pakistani airspace. According to Peter Bergen, the raid was "constantly 'red-teamed'" to simulate defenses the SEALs had encountered in other, similar situations: "armed women, people with suicide jackets hidden under their pajamas, insurgents hiding in 'spider holes,' and even buildings entirely rigged with explosives." By the end of the exercise, one colleague observed, "McRaven had a backup for every possible failure, and a backup to the failure of the backup, and a backup to the failure of the backup of the backup."

It's true that people naturally attempt to anticipate objections or possible failure points when they contemplate challenging decisions. The expression "let's play devil's advocate for a second" is often heard in conference rooms and casual conversations. The difference with strategies like premortems and red teams lies in the formal nature of the process: giving people a specific task and identity to role-play. It's not enough to ask someone, "Can you think of any way this plan might fail?" Premortems and red teams force you to take on a new perspective, or consider an alternate narrative, that might not easily come to mind in a few minutes of casual devil's advocacy. In a way, the process is similar to the strategy of assigning expert roles that we explored in the mapping stage of the decision. By taking on a new identity, seeing the world through a simulated worldview, new outcomes become visible.

Experimenting with different identities is more than just a way of uncovering new opportunities or pitfalls. Hard choices are often hard because they impact other people's lives in meaningful ways, and so our ability to imagine that impact—to think through the emotional and material consequences from someone else's perspective—turns out to be an essential talent. New research suggests that this kind of psychological projection is part of what the brain's default network does in daydreaming. When we simulate potential futures in our wandering minds, we often shift the mental camera from one consciousness to another without even realizing it, testing different scenarios and the emotional reactions they might provoke. You're driving to work and thinking about a new job opportunity, and your mind flashes onto the image of your boss responding to the news. It's a fantasy, a simulation, because it's an event that hasn't happened yet. But the work that goes into that fantasy is truly sublime. You're mapping out all the reasons why you might reasonably be considering leaving your current job *and* you're mapping out all the reasons why your boss might be alarmed or hurt (or both) at the news, and you're building a mental forecast of what kind of response the collision of those two maps might trigger in him. That is a very rich and complicated form of mental simulation, but we run those calculations so fast we don't appreciate them.

Still, some of us do it better than others. And that ability to shift our imagination between different perspectives may be one of the core attributes of a farsighted mind. Part of being a smart decision-maker is being open-minded enough to realize that other people might have a different way of thinking about the decision. Recall Lydgate contemplating the way small-minded Middlemarch gossip would respond to his choice of which vicar to support. Lydgate himself is above the gossip, but he is far-sighted enough to realize that the approbation of the town will make a meaningful difference if he makes the wrong choice, given that his practice as a local physician depends on being well-regarded by the community. Lydgate's mind shifts effortlessly from the self-centric question "Which candidate do I like the most?" to an external frame of reference: "What will the town gossips think of me if I choose my patron's candidate to be the vicar?" In that moment, he is running a rough simulation not just of the consequences of his choice, but something more remarkable: a simulation of other minds, with their own quirks and obsessions and values.

This shifting of perspective played a key role in what was arguably the most impressive bit of long-term scenario planning in the hunt for bin Laden. An attack on a private compound raised a huge number of logistical questions: How do we determine who is inside? Should we capture or kill bin Laden? But it also raised a question that required the team to venture outside their default American perspective: What will the Pakistanis think if we launch an attack inside their borders without alerting them first? While a coordinated attack with Pakistani forces was still being considered, it was generally thought to be the least appealing option, given the risk of the plan leaking out in some fashion and alerting bin Laden that his hideout had been compromised. A stealth attack by Black Hawks through Pakistani airspace posed a different kind of risk. First, the helicopters might be detected— and potentially shot down—by Pakistani forces, though McRaven and his team believed they could get in and out without Pakistani patrols noticing them. The real risk was the downstream one. Pakistan, after all, was at least nominally an ally of the United States in the war on terror. The United States relied heavily on the good graces of the Pakistani government to get supplies into landlocked Afghanistan. More than three hundred daily flights by US planes, delivering supplies and personnel to American and NATO troops in Afghanistan, were permitted over Pakistani territory. Once the Pakistanis discovered the United States had invaded their airspace to attack a suburban residence without their permission—particularly if the residence turned out *not* to be the home of a certain terrorist ringleader—it was an open question whether they would continue to grant America and its allies the same access.

On March 21, 2011, weeks before McRaven began his simulated attacks at Fort Bragg and months before Obama made the final decision to send in SEAL Team 6, defense secretary Robert Gates announced a new partnership to strengthen the so-called Northern Distribution Network, a route into Afghanistan running from ports on the Baltic Sea through Russia and other countries—a route that, crucially, bypasses Pakistan altogether. No one realized it at the time, but that expanded distribution network was a direct result of the perspective-shifting scenario planning behind the bin Laden raid. Even if they got their man, the administration realized that the downstream effects on Pakistan-US relations might be catastrophic, which would threaten a vital route relied on by the United States and allied troops immersed in active combat. And so they took the time to ensure that another route would be available if that scenario did, in fact, come to pass.

In the end, the predictive exercises that shaped the bin Laden mission turned out to be as full spectrum as the mapping exercises. To build a coherent set of scenarios, it was necessary to think like a meteorologist, assessing the impact of the desert heat and altitude on the helicopters. They had to study the smallest architectural details of the compound to determine how the SEALs could successfully get inside. They had to wrestle with the juridical question of whether and where to hold a trial for bin Laden if he were captured alive. They had to imagine the conspiracy theories and folklore that might erupt if al-Qaeda's leader were immolated in a B-2 bombing run, leaving no proof of his demise. They had to put themselves in the shoes of the Pakistani government and imagine what kind of response a violation of their airspace might engender. They collected DNA from bin Laden's relatives so they would have genetic evidence to identify his remains. They even had to study Islamic burial rituals so that they could dispose of bin Laden's body in a way that would not outrage moderate Muslims. Air pressure, international law, religious customs, the slant of a roof, genetic fingerprints, geopolitical backlash—all these variables and more found their way into the scenarios plotted in the late spring of 2011. They'd told stories that imagined different outcomes; they'd assembled red teams to challenge their assumptions. By early May, the divergence of all these different perspectives and possibilities had reached their logical limits. The decision had been mapped, the options identified, the scenarios planned. It was time to decide.

3

DECIDING

Mapping, predicting, simulating: they don't quite add up to *deciding*. Once you've mapped the landscape, determined a full range of potential options, and simulated the outcomes for those options with as much certainty as you can—how, then, do you choose?

Ever since Ben Franklin outlined his "moral algebra" to Joseph Priestley, people have concocted increasingly elaborate systems for adjudicating decisions based on some kind of calculation. Priestley himself played a defining role in one of the most influential of these strategies. A few years before he wrote his letter to Franklin, Priestley published a political treatise that suggested a different approach for making the final call on group decisions, like the creation of laws and regulations: "It must necessarily be understood," Priestley wrote, "that all people live in society for their mutual advantage; so that the good and happiness of the members, that is the majority of the members of any state, is the great standard by which every thing relating to that state must finally be determined." A few decades later, the line would plant the seed of an idea in the mind of the political philosopher

Jeremy Bentham, who used it as the cornerstone of the utilitarian ideology that would become one of the most influential political ideas of the nineteenth century. Moral decisions—both public and private—should be based on actions that produced the "greatest happiness for the greatest number," in Bentham's famous phrase. The problem of doing good in the world was a problem that could, in theory at least, be solved by doing a kind of emotional census of all those connected to a given choice.

The "greatest happiness for the greatest number" sounds like a vague platitude, but Bentham's aim was to try to calculate those values with as much precision as possible. At first, he divided our experience of the world into two broad categories:

> *Nature has placed mankind under the governance of two sovereign masters, pain and pleasure. It is for them alone to point out what we ought to do, as well as to determine what we shall do. On the one hand the standard of right and wrong, on the other the chain of causes and effects, are fastened to their throne. They govern us in all we do, in all we say, in all we think: every effort we can make to throw off our subjection, will serve but to demonstrate and confirm it.*

Bentham ultimately recognized that there were subcategories of pain and pleasure that would have to be brought into the equation: the intensity of pain or pleasure, the duration of the experience, how certain the outcome was, the proximity of the pain or pleasure to the action that triggered it, the "fecundity" of the experience—in other words, the likelihood that it would trigger more experiences of pain or pleasure—the purity of the experience, and the sheer number of people affected by the decision. A utilitarian confronted a decision by building a kind of mental map of all the waves of pain and pleasure that would ripple out from the various options under discussion. The moral choice would be the one that led to the greatest increase in the sum total of human happiness.

The clarity of that formula—like the rational choice of classical economics—necessarily grows cloudy when confronted with actual decisions in the world, for all the reasons we have explored. It is easy to imagine why Bentham (and John Stuart Mill, his fellow utilitarian) might have imagined this kind of emotional census would be possible. The first century or two of the Enlightenment had demonstrated how powerful and illuminating new ways of measuring the world could be. Why couldn't the same rational approach be applied to the choices that individual human beings and societies confront? The problem, of course, is the problem of bounded rationality that Herbert Simon observed more than a century later: hard choices send waves out into the world that are difficult to map and predict in advance, particularly when the calculation involves the future happiness of thousands or millions of people.

But while the utilitarians might have been overly optimistic in thinking that those outcomes could be clearly measured, the truth is, we rely on the descendants of that moral calculation in many facets of modern life. In the United States, one of the most influential of those descendants was put into place on February 17, 1981, when Ronald Reagan signed Executive Order 12291 as one of the first actions of his administration. EO 12291 mandated that every new rule or regulation proposed by any agency of the government undergo what was called a "regulatory impact analysis." By law, the analysis had to include:

1. *A description of the potential benefits of the rule, including any beneficial effects that cannot be quantified in monetary terms, and the identification of those likely to receive the benefits;*

2. *A description of the potential costs of the rule, including any adverse effects that cannot be quantified in monetary terms, and the identification of those likely to bear the costs;*

3. *A determination of the potential net benefits of the rule, including an evaluation of effects that cannot be quantified in monetary terms;*

4. *A description of alternative approaches that could substantially achieve the same regulatory goal at lower cost, together with an analysis of this potential benefit and costs and a brief explanation of the legal reasons why such alternatives, if proposed, could not be adopted.*

Regulatory impact analysis was, in practice, what we commonly call cost-benefit analysis. In deciding whether to implement a new regulation, agencies would have to calculate the potential costs and benefits of the regulation, in part by predicting the downstream consequences of implementing it. The executive order effectively compelled government agencies, eventually overseen by the Office of Information and Regulatory Affairs (OIRA), to walk through the key steps of decision-making that we have explored—mapping all the potential variables and predicting the long-term effects—*and* it even pushed them to explore other decision paths that might not have been initially visible when the proposed regulation was originally being drafted. If, at the end of the analysis, the regulation could be shown to "maximize net benefits"—in other words, not just do more good than harm, but do more good than any other comparable option on the table—the agency would be free to implement it. "Reagan's ideas applied across a spectacularly wide range, covering regulations meant to protect the environment, increase food safety, reduce risks on the highways and in the air, promote health care, improve immigration, affect the energy supply, or increase homeland security," writes Cass Sunstein, who ran OIRA for several years during the Obama administration.

When it was first proposed, regulatory impact analysis was seen as a conservative intervention, an attempt to rein in runaway government spending. But the basic framework has persevered, largely unmodified, through six administrations. It is one of the rarest of creatures in the Washington ecosystem: an institutional practice with bipartisan support that leads to better government. Cost-benefit analysis turned out to have genuine potential as a tool for progressive values, and not just anti–Big Government cutbacks. Under the Obama administration, an interagency group formulated a monetary figure measuring "the social cost of carbon"—a cost that many environmentalists felt had been long overlooked in our decisions about energy policy. Experts were drawn from the Council on Environmental Quality, the National Economic Council, the Office of Energy and Climate Change, the Office of Science and Technology Policy, the EPA, and the Departments of Agriculture, Commerce, Energy, Transportation, and Treasury. Collectively, they mapped all the downstream effects of releasing carbon into the atmosphere, from agriculture disruptions triggered by climate changes to the economic cost of increasingly severe weather events to the geographic dislocation triggered by rising sea levels. In the end, they calculated the social cost of carbon to be $36 per ton released into the atmosphere.

The figure itself was only an estimate—a more recent Stanford study suggests it may be several times higher—but it provided a baseline cost for any government regulation that involved carbon-generating technology. The calculation, for instance, was an essential justification for the aggressive targets for fuel economy standards that the EPA mandated for automobiles and trucks during the Obama administration. In a sense, by assigning a dollar value to the cost of carbon, regulators were adding a predictive stage to decisions that involved fossil fuels, one that offered a long-term view. Their decision was no longer limited to the present-tense benefit of using those fuels as a source of energy. That $36/ton cost gave them a way of measuring the future impact of the decision as well. It was, at its core, a calculation: If we choose this option, how much carbon will that release into the atmosphere, and how much will it cost for us to deal with the consequences of those emissions in the years to come? But that calculation made the choice far more farsighted than it would have been without it.

THE VALUE MODEL

The ultimate output of a regulatory impact analysis is a financial statement—the net costs and benefits reported in dollars—but the original executive order did recognize that not all effects could be quantified in purely monetary terms, and subsequent changes have made the formal analysis more sensitive to noneconomic outcomes. Within the government, this has led to some thorny economic translations, most famously the question of how agencies should appropriately measure the cost of a human life. (As it happens, OIRA values a single human life at approximately

$9 million in its regulatory analyses.) If this seems inhumane, keep in mind that the government is forced to make tradeoffs every day that clearly result in the deaths of human beings. We would certainly save thousands of lives every year if we universally set the speed limit at 25 mph, but we have decided, as a society, that the transportation and commercial benefits that come from higher speed limits are "worth" the cost in traffic fatalities.

Other descendants of Bentham's equation do not rely exclusively on monetary assessments. One heavily mathematical approach goes by the name "linear value modeling" (LVM), and it is employed widely in making astute planning decisions like the one the citizens of New York failed to make with the destruction of Collect Pond. The formula goes something like this: Once you have mapped the decision, explored alternative options, and built a predictive model of outcomes, you then write down a list of the values that are most important to you. Think back to Darwin's personal choice of whether to marry. His values included freedom, companionship, the clever conversation of men at clubs, having children, and many others. Just as Franklin suggested in his original description of the pros-vs.-cons list, a values model requires that you give each of those values a weight, a measure of their relative importance to you. (Darwin, for instance, seems to have valued the promise of lifelong companionship and children more highly than the clever men in the clubs.) In the most mathematical version of this approach, you give each value a weight somewhere between 0 and 1. If the clever conversation is secondary to you, you give it a .25, while the prospect of having children might get a .90.

With the values properly weighted, you then turn to the scenarios you've developed for each of the options on the table, and you effectively grade each option in terms of how it addresses your core values. Grade that on the scale of 1 to 100. Remaining a bachelor scores very poorly on the "having children" value, but does better on the clever conversation front. Once you've established those grades for each scenario, you then do some elemental math: multiply each grade by the weight of each value and add up the numbers for each scenario. The scenario with the highest score wins. Had Darwin built a values model for his decision, the ledger might have looked like this:

VALUES	WEIGHTS	SCENARIO A: UNMARRIED	SCENARIO B: MARRIED
Lack of quarreling	.25	80	30
Children	.75	0	70
Freedom	.25	80	10
Lower expenses	.50	100	10
Clever men in clubs	.10	80	40
Lifelong companion	.75	10	100

Adjusted by weight, the grades for each scenario look like this:

VALUES	WEIGHTS	SCENARIO A: UNMARRIED	SCENARIO B: MARRIED
Lack of quarreling	.25	20	7.5
Children	.75	0	52.5
Freedom	.25	20	2.5
Lower expenses	.50	50	5
Clever men in clubs	.10	8	4
Lifelong companion	.75	7.5	75

The result would have been the same as the one that Darwin eventually arrived at: a decisive victory for marriage—144.5 to

105.5—despite the fact that the bachelor option had higher grades for more than half the values.

Franklin called his approach "moral algebra," but values modeling is closer to a moral *algorithm*: a series of instructions for manipulating data that generates a result, in this case a numerical rating for the various options being considered. I suspect many of us will find this kind of calculation to be too reductive, taking a complex, emotional decision and compressing it down to a mathematical formula. But, of course, the whole process is dependent on the many steps that have preceded it: mapping the decision, imagining scenarios, conducting premortems, and holding charrettes. The weights and grades only work if they're calculated at the end of a full-spectrum investigation of the choice at hand. Still, the same framework can be applied without actually doing the math: list your core values, think about their relative importance to you, sketch out how each scenario might impact those values, and, based on that more narrative exercise, make your decision.

In situations where the choice involves more than two options, LVM practitioners often find this approach is especially useful as a tool for eliminating weaker scenarios. Something about tallying up the numbers has a tendency to shine a particularly unforgiving light on a choice that fares poorly on almost all the metrics. (In the lingo, these are called "dominated" alternatives.) In the end, you might not make the ultimate choice for the two top rivals based exclusively on the numbers, but the numbers might have helped you pare down the list to just two alternatives worth considering. The values calculation helps you prune, after spending so much time growing alternative branches.

In a way, the value-modeling approach is a descendant of

Bentham and Mill's "greatest happiness for the greatest number," though at first glance, it might seem to be a more self-
centered rendition of their moral calculus. But the values model
needn't be oriented exclusively around one's personal interests
and objectives. To begin with, the decision doesn't have to be
based on a single person's values. In fact, value modeling turns
out to be particularly useful for dealing with a decision where the
stakeholders have competing values, because you can do calculations with different weights corresponding to the different perspectives of all the stakeholders. Darwin's pros-vs.-cons ledger
doesn't easily scale up to the competing demands of a community. But the linear value modeling approach does. And, of
course, the values you prioritize don't have to be self-centered,
either. If you give a high weight to "improving the well-being of
the growing city of Manhattan by building a park," by definition
you bring a "greater number" into your calculations—greater, at
least, than the small circle of your immediate family.

The fact that these sorts of calculations can help us make
more farsighted decisions raises one intriguing possibility. If
we're going to use mathematical algorithms in our deliberative
process, what happens when we try to run these calculations in a
machine whose native language is algorithmic?

RISK MAGNITUDE

In May 2012, Google filed patent #8781669 with the US
Patent Office. The filing had an unlikely name for a company
that had made its name filtering web searches: "Consideration of
risks in active sensing for an autonomous vehicle." The filing

turned out to be one of the first public acknowledgments that Google was exploring self-driving cars.

The patent filing outlines a long series of technical interactions between sensors, supplemented by diagrams of where those sensors are positioned on the car. But at its core, it is a description of how an autonomous vehicle would make difficult decisions. The filing contains a fascinating table, outlining exactly how the software controlling the car would consider risk when confronted with a dangerous situation on the road: A pedestrian jumps into your lane on a two-way street with oncoming traffic. What should the car decide to do?

At first glance, that kind of choice might seem less pertinent to the subject matter of this book, given that these are the very antithesis of deliberative decisions for humans. At 40 mph, to deliberate for even a half second is effectively not to choose at all, because you will have already collided with the pedestrian before you settle on a path. But computers work at different speeds: faster at some things, slower (or flat-out incompetent) at others. One of those faster things is running through the spatial geometry—and physics—of a system with a moderate number of meaningful variables: a body walking through an intersection; an SUV hurtling toward you. Because those kinds of problems can be solved—though "solved" isn't quite the right word for it, as we will see—at seemingly miraculous speeds, digital decision-making algorithms can condense some of the techniques that we have explored for farsighted decisions into a few nanoseconds. That's why the table included in Google's patent bears a meaningful resemblance to the tables of linear values modeling. Google's self-driving car can shrink deliberation down to the speed of instinct.

The table is a list of "bad events." Some are catastrophic:

getting hit by a truck, running over a pedestrian. Some are minor: losing information from a sensor on the car because it's blocked by some object. Each bad event is scored with two key attributes: risk magnitude and probability. If the car barely crosses the median, there's a low probability that it will collide with an oncoming car, but that collision itself would have high risk magnitude. If it swerves into the parking lane, the angle might obscure one of the cameras, but the likelihood of a high-magnitude collision might be reduced to zero. From these assessments, the software calculates a "risk penalty" for each action by multiplying a risk magnitude by the probability. Getting hit by an oncoming vehicle might be extremely unlikely (.01 percent), but the magnitude of the risk is so high that the software steers away from options that might lead to that outcome, even if many of the other "bad events" are more than a thousand times more likely to happen.

BAD EVENT	RISK MAGNITUDE	PROBABILITY (%)	RISK PENALTY
Getting hit by a large truck	5,000	0.01%	0.5
Getting hit by an oncoming vehicle	20,000	0.01%	2
Getting hit from behind by a vehicle approaching in the left-hand lane	10,000	0.03%	3
Hitting a pedestrian who runs into the middle of the road	100,000	0.001%	1
Losing information that is provided by the camera in current position	10	10%	1
Losing information that is provided by other sensor in current position	2	25%	0.5
Interference with path planning involving right turn at traffic light	50	100% (if turn is planned)	50/0

As the car confronts a dynamic situation on the road, it rapidly assembles multiple versions of this table, based on the potential actions it can take: swerving left, swerving right, slamming on the brakes, and so on. Each action contains a different set of probabilities for all the potential risks. Swerving right away from oncoming traffic reduces the risk of a head-on collision to almost zero, but still leaves a meaningful possibility that you'll collide with the pedestrian. The risk magnitude scores are effectively the car's moral compass, a distant descendant of Bentham's utilitarian analysis: it is better to interfere with path planning for an upcoming right turn than it is to run over a pedestrian, because the former will lead to greater good for the greater number, particularly that pedestrian. In the Bad Events Table, the moral code is expressed numerically: in this example, the software assumes running over a pedestrian is five times worse than colliding with an oncoming vehicle—presumably because the car is traveling at a speed where the pedestrian would likely die, but the occupants of both cars would survive the collision. At higher speeds, the risk magnitudes would be different.

The Bad Events Table is a kind of mirror-image version of the values model. Our values model reconstruction of Darwin's pros-vs.-cons list created weights for all the positive outcomes he wished to achieve in life: clever conversation, a family, companionship. The Google table creates weights for all the negative outcomes, and it modifies those weights with probability assessments. Although it was designed to make split-second decisions, the structure of the Bad Events Table has important lessons for human beings making deliberative decisions about events that might unfold over months or years. For starters, it deliberately includes the kind of probability assessments that were so important to the internal debate over the bin Laden raid. And it forces us to consider not just our objectives and values, but also something we can be too quick to dismiss: the highly unlikely catastrophe. Some outcomes are so disastrous that it's prudent to avoid them at any cost, even if their likelihood is slim. Taking the time to generate your own Bad Events Table for a complex decision you're mulling over keeps your mind from focusing exclusively on the upside.

Uncertainty, as Herbert Simon famously demonstrated, is an inevitable factor in any complex decision, however farsighted the decision-maker might be. If we had perfect clairvoyance about the downstream consequences of our choices, we wouldn't need all the strategies of premortems and scenario plans to help us imagine the future. But there are ways to mitigate that uncertainty in the act of deciding. The first is to avoid the tendency to focus exclusively on the most likely outcome. When people are lucky enough to hit upon an option that seems likely to generate the best possible results, given all the variables at play, they naturally tend to fixate on that path and not think about the less likely outcomes that reside within the cone of uncertainty. A decision path where there's a 70 percent chance of arriving at a great outcome but a 30 percent chance of a disastrous one is a very different kind of choice from one where the 30 percent chance is not ideal, but is tolerable. And so part of the art of deciding lies in making peace with the less likely outcome as a failsafe measure. McRaven and his team had good reason to believe that the Pakistanis would ultimately understand why the Americans felt the need to invade their airspace without warning during the bin Laden raid, but they also recognized that their allies might see the raid as a betrayal and seek some kind of retribution.

And so they established the alternate supply route to the troops in Afghanistan as a way of getting comfortable with that potential outcome. But if there's no way around the second most likely outcome being a catastrophic one, it's probably time to go back and look for another path forward.

Another way of mitigating uncertainty is to favor paths that allow modifications after you've embarked on them. Decision paths vary in terms of how much you can tinker with them *after* you've committed to one path over another. A path that promises a great outcome 70 percent of the time but doesn't allow further iteration once you've made the final choice may, in the end, be less desirable than a decision that allows you to modify it after the fact. This is, in a sense, a version of the "minimally viable product" idea that is so fashionable in the tech sector today: Don't try to ship the perfect product; ship the simplest product that might possibly be useful to your customer, and then refine and improve it once it's out in the market. Thinking about a decision this way suggests a different variable to add to the linear values model: downstream flexibility. Moving to a new town and buying a house has less downstream flexibility than moving to a new town and renting. The third option that Darwin didn't dare include on his pros-vs.-cons list—move in with with Emma without marrying and see how they get along before tying the knot—has become far more commonplace today, precisely because it gives you more flexibility if things don't go as planned in the future. If there are paths on the table that allow that kind of downstream flexibility, they might well be the most strategic ones to take, given the uncertainty and complexity of the future. We have a tendency to value the decisive leader, the one who makes a hard choice and sticks with it. But sometimes the most farsighted decisions are the ones that leave room for tinkering down the line.

MULLING

As rich as the history of computational decision-making may be—from Bentham to Google's self-driving car—I think it's fair to say that most of us end up making complex decisions without actually doing any math. This is probably not a bad thing. The most important work lies in the way we frame the decision, the strategies we use to overcome all the challenges of bounded rationality: exploring multiple perspectives, building scenario plans, identifying new options. If we've done a thorough job working through the mapping and predicting phases, the actual choice often becomes self-evident. This, too, is one of those places where the brain's default network is so important. Your mind is amazingly gifted at mulling over a complicated decision, imagining how it might affect other people, imagining how you yourself might respond to different outcomes. We all make those intuitive scenario plans as a background process with extraordinary skill. The problem is that our visibility is often limited when we create those scenarios, so we miss crucial variables, or we get stuck in one assumption about how events will likely transpire, or we fail to see a third option that might actually reconcile conflicting objectives. So the mapping and predicting stages of a complex choice are really about giving the default network more material to process.

You can map all the variables, "red team" your assumptions, and build scenario plans for different options, but in the end, the final decision usually turns out to be closer to art than science. All the exercises of mapping and predicting—and the diversity of perspectives brought into the conversation—can open up new possible options that weren't visible at the outset, or help you see why your first instincts were the wrong ones, the way the Obama team slowly came to see the possibility that the compound might indeed be housing their archenemy. If you're lucky, investing the time and contemplation into the decision process takes you to a place where the choice becomes clear.

But sometimes the answer is murkier, and you have to make the tough call between a few remaining options, each of which promises a different mix of pain and pleasure to the individuals affected by the choice. In those situations, keeping score can sometimes be clarifying—as in the linear values approach. It can certainly help to think about the decision in computational terms if you are making group choices that involve different stakeholders with different objectives and values. But for choices with a small number of decision-makers, the best approach is often an old-fashioned one: give your mind the free time to mull it over. In a sense, the preparation for the choice should involve state-of-the-art strategies: premortems, scenario plans, expert roles, stakeholder charrettes. But once those exercises have widened your perspective and helped you escape your initial gut reactions, the next step is to let it all sink in and let the default network do its magic. Go for long walks, linger in the shower a little longer than usual, let your mind wander.

Hard choices demand that we train the mind to override the snap judgments of System 1 thinking, that we keep our mind open to new possibilities—starting with the possibility that our instinctive response to a situation is quite likely the wrong one.

Almost every strategy described in this book ultimately pursues the same objective: helping you to see the current situation from new perspectives, to push against the limits of bounded rationality, to make a list of things that would never occur to you. These are not, strictly speaking, solutions to the problem you confront. They are prompts, hacks, nudges. They're designed to get you outside your default assumptions, not to give you a fixed answer. But unlike the quack cures that Darwin dabbled in—along with the rest of the Victorians—many of these interventions have been supported and refined by controlled experiments. We don't have an infallible algorithm for making wise choices, but we do have a meaningful body of techniques that can keep us from making stupid ones.

OBAMA'S CHOICE

When word first reached Washington about the strange compound on the edge of Abbottabad that al-Kuwaiti had been tracked to, almost everyone who heard the description of the residence had the same instinctive reaction: it didn't seem like the kind of place Osama bin Laden would use as a hideout. But those gut feelings, as powerful as they must have seemed at the time, turned out to be wrong, just as the sense that Saddam Hussein *must* be working on some kind of WMD program turned out to be wrong as well. But because the intelligence community and the White House did not merely submit to their instincts about bin Laden, but instead probed and challenged them; because they took a full-spectrum approach to mapping both the decision of whether bin Laden was living in the compound *and* the decision of how to attack it;

because they built long-term predictions about the consequences of that attack and "red-teamed" those predictions—because, more than anything, they thought of the decision as a process that required time and collaboration and structured deliberation, they were able to see past the distortions of their initial instincts and make the right choice.

Neither Obama nor his direct reports appear to have done a mathematical analysis of the bin Laden decision, other than the many times they estimated the probability of bin Laden being in the compound. But in every other sense, they followed the patterns of decision-making that we have explored over the preceding chapters. In the end, Obama gathered his key team and asked each one to weigh in on the decision. Only Vice President Biden and Defense Secretary Gates voted against going in. Everyone else supported the raid, even though many—including Obama himself—thought the odds were fifty-fifty at best that they would find bin Laden on the premises. Gates would change his mind the next day; Biden remained opposed, and would later declare that Obama had "*cojones* of steel" for overruling his vice president and giving the green light to the raid. As is so often the case, by exploring the decision, playing out all the future consequences, and letting the default network do its work, it had become increasingly clear that one path led in the most promising direction. As the team investigated the four main options for attacking the compound, fatal flaws surfaced for three options—bombing runs, a targeted drone strike, and collaboration with the Pakistanis—leaving McRaven's plan for the raid the last choice standing.

There was no shortage of praise for the killing of the al Qaeda leader once the news was announced. It was, in the end, a rare thing in the world of espionage and counterterror operations: an unqualified success. The compound did, in fact, turn out to be the home of Osama bin Laden; in a brief firefight, bin Laden was killed and his body removed; the SEALs suffered only minor injuries. The only factor McRaven and his team had not properly mapped was the internal wind currents in the courtyard that destabilized one of the Black Hawks as it attempted to land, causing it to crash. But even the possibility of losing one chopper was part of the scenario planning; they had ensured that the team could all reassemble on a single Black Hawk after the raid was completed. The loss of the chopper was a known unknown: you could plan for it, since it seemed within the realm of possibility that *something* would cause a Black Hawk to crash near the grounds. When that possible scenario became a reality, the SEALs followed the plan they had simulated in the months leading up to the raid: they blew it up, and then moved on.

What do we typically celebrate when an operation like this goes well? We celebrate the courage of both the SEAL Team 6 unit and their commanders. We celebrate the decisiveness of our leaders and their intelligence in making the right choice. But these are all attributes, not actions. What made the bin Laden decision such a successful one, in the end, was the way it was approached as a problem. There was intelligence and courage and decisiveness, to be sure, but those attributes had also been on display in less successful military actions like the Battle of Brooklyn or the Bay of Pigs. There were brilliant, confident minds making the decisions during the Iran hostage rescue mission and the Iraq WMD investigation. What this team had was different: a deliberation process that forced them to investigate all the things they didn't like about the evidence and imagine all the ways their course of action could go terribly wrong. That process mattered every bit as much as the actual execution of the raid. But that process tends to get lost in the public memory of the event, because the heroism and the spectacular violence of a moonlit raid naturally overwhelm the subtleties of the months and months spent probing the decision itself. We should want our leaders—in government, in civic life, in corporate board-rooms, on planning commissions—to show that same willing-ness to slow down the decision, approach it from multiple angles, and challenge their instincts. If we are going to learn from triumphs like the Abbottabad raid, the raid itself is less important than the decision process that made it possible.

When the Black Hawks landed in Jalalabad at two in the morning, carrying the body of Osama bin Laden, McRaven and the CIA station chief laid out the body to do a proper identifica-tion. They realized, after all their planning, that they had failed to secure a tape measure to confirm that the body was six foot four, the known height of bin Laden. (They ultimately found someone the same height, who lay down next to the body so they could get a rough measurement.) Several weeks later, President Obama presented McRaven with a plaque praising him for his acumen in planning the mission. The plaque featured a tape mea-sure mounted to its surface, a reminder of one of the very few ele-ments that the "McRaven option" had failed to anticipate. McRaven and the rest of the analysts had mapped the decision and all of its complexity with astonishing detail and foresight; they had measured the compound and its walls down to the inch. They just forgot to bring a device to measure bin Laden himself.

4

THE GLOBAL CHOICE

What happens fast is illusion, what happens slowly is
reality. The job of the long view is to penetrate illusion.

• STEWART BRAND

In the early 1960s, during the craze for war games that
shaped so much of Cold War military strategy, the Naval
War College acquired a $10 million computer. Its purpose
was not to calculate torpedo trajectories or to help plan ship-
building budgets. It was, instead, a game machine known as the
Naval Electronic War Simulator. By managing the simulations of
war games, the computer could amplify the decision-making
powers of the military commanders, since a computer could presumably model a much more complex set of relationships than a
bunch of humans rolling dice and moving tokens around a game
board. It is unclear whether the Naval Electronic War Simulator
actually improved US military decision-making in the years that
followed. Certainly, the ultimate path of the Vietnam War suggests that its intelligence amplification was limited at best.

The idea of a computer smart enough to assist with complex
decisions may have been premature in the 1960s, but today it no

longer seems like science fiction. Ensemble forecasts from meteorological supercomputers help us decide whether to evacuate a coastal area threatened by a hurricane. Cities use urban simulators to evaluate the traffic or economic impact of building new bridges, subways, or highways. The decisions that confounded some of the finest minds of the nineteenth century—the urban planners filling in Collect Pond, Darwin and his water cure—are increasingly being guided by algorithms and virtual worlds.

Supercomputers have started taking on the role that in ancient times belonged to the oracles: they allow us to peer into the future. As that foresight grows more powerful, we rely on these machines more and more to assist us in our hard choices, and perhaps even to make them for us. It's easy enough to imagine computer simulations and forecasts helping to decide the future of Collect Pond: projecting population growth in downtown Manhattan, the ecosystem impact of destroying a freshwater resource, and the economic fortunes of the tanneries polluting that water.

Almost a hundred years ago, when Lewis Fry Richardson alluded in his "Weather Prediction by Numerical Process" essay to the "dream" of a machine that might someday be able to calculate weather forecasts, the mathematician had only imagined predictions that extended a few days into the future, far enough perhaps to bring ships into harbor before a hurricane or prepare a bustling city for a coming blizzard. Richardson would no doubt be amazed to see the state of "numerical processing" two decades into the twenty-first century: machines like the supercomputer "Cheyenne" housed in the Wyoming offices of the National Center for Atmospheric Research, which uses its vast computational power to simulate the behavior of Earth's climate itself. Machines like Cheyenne allow us to simulate time scales that would have seemed

preposterous to Richardson: decades, even centuries. The forecasts are fuzzier, of course: you can't ask Cheyenne to tell you
whether New Yorkers should dress for rain on July 13, 2087. They
can only tell us long-term trends—where new deserts may form,
where floods may become more likely, where ice caps may melt—
and even those are just probabilities. But that foresight, hazy as it
may sometimes seem, is far more accurate than anything Richardson could have imagined just a century ago.

Digital technology is often blamed for the abbreviated attention spans of Snapchat and Twitter, but the fact is that computer
simulations have been essential in forcing humans to confront
what may be the most complex, long-term decision we have ever
faced: what to do about climate change. The near-universal consensus among scientists that global warming poses a meaningful
threat has emerged, in large part, thanks to the simulations of
supercomputers like Cheyenne. Without the full-spectrum models that those machines are capable of building—tracking everything from planet-scale phenomena like the jet stream all the way
down to the molecular properties of carbon dioxide—we would
have far less confidence about the potential danger from climate
change and the long-term importance of shifting to renewable
energy sources. Those simulations now influence millions of decisions all across the planet, from individual choices to buy a hybrid
automobile instead of a gas-powered one and community decisions to install solar panels to power public schools all the way up
to decisions on the scale of signing the Paris climate accord, truly
one of the most global agreements—both in its signatories and its
objectives—ever reached in the history of our species.

The fact that we are capable of making these decisions should
not be an excuse to rest on our laurels. I am writing these words

in the fall of 2017, just a few months after the Trump administration announced that the United States would be withdrawing from the Paris Agreement. It is possible that we will look back at this period twenty or thirty years from now and see this as the beginning of a great unraveling, with more and more citizens dismissing climate change as "fake news," generating increasing paralysis on a governmental level, and undermining efforts to reduce the impact of global warming.

If you polled most Americans, I suspect a majority of them would say that we are getting *worse* at long-term decisions, that we live in a short-attention-span age that keeps us from the long view. A significant number would probably point to the damage we are doing as a species to the environment as the most conspicuous example of our shortsightedness.

It is true that the last few decades have witnessed a number of troubling trends, most of which revolve around that critical attribute of diversity, that have compromised the way we make collective decisions in material ways. In the United States, gerrymandering reduces the ideological diversity behind the decision of who to elect to represent a district in the House of Representatives: members of Congress are increasingly elected by voting blocs that are overwhelmingly Republican or Democratic, far more homogeneous in their political worldviews than most congressional districts would have been at other points of our history. But that trend is not solely attributable to the schemes of politicians trying to ensure reelection. We are also experiencing a demographic "Big Sort," in which our cities and inner-ring suburbs are increasingly populated by Democrats, while Republicans dominate the exurbs and the countryside. So when we come together to make any kind of local decision, we are—politically, at least—assembling teams of decision-makers that are more homogeneous and thus prone to all the failings that homogeneity brings to group decisions.

This is an often underappreciated point in the cultural debates about the importance of diversity. When we look at those images of a Trump cabinet meeting or the Republican House Caucus—all those middle-aged white men in their suits and ties—we tend to frame the lack of diversity in those groups as a problem for egalitarian or representational reasons. And that's a perfectly valid framing. We want a cabinet that "looks like America" because that will get us closer to a world where talented people from all walks of life can find their way into the top echelons of government, and because those different walks of life will inevitably have different interests that will need to be reflected in the way we are governed. But there is another factor that we often ignore when we complain about the lack of diversity at the top of any organization in the private or public sector: *Diverse groups make smarter decisions.* Nowhere is the data on this clearer than in the research on gender and decision-making. If you were trying to assemble a kind of *Springtime for Hitler* anti–dream team, designed to *fail* at complex decisions, you would do well to recruit an all-male roster. So when we see a phalanx of guys signing a bill to block funding to Planned Parenthood, we should not just point out that a woman might have an understanding of Planned Parenthood's value that a man might lack. We should also point out that a group of men is more likely to make the wrong choice about *anything*, not just "women's issues."

But despite those limitations and setbacks, we should remind ourselves that in many other realms, we are attempting to make decisions that involve time horizons and full-spectrum maps that would have been unthinkable to our great-grandparents. No one in

1960 made a decision that contemplated for even a second that decision's impact on atmospheric carbon in 2060. Today, countless people around the globe make decisions that factor in those long-term impacts every single day, from politicians proposing new regulations that include the true cost of carbon in their cost-benefit analysis and corporate executives choosing to run their headquarters on renewable energy sources all the way down to ordinary consumers who choose to buy "green" products at the supermarket.

Think back to Meadow Lake in Queens and those fish struggling to find oxygen beneath the superbloom of blue-green algae. Those fish were, in a sense, stakeholders in the decision process. They were included as a meaningful variable in part because they play an important role in the ecosystem, which ultimately sustains life for human beings, but also because many of us believe they have some intrinsic right to life as a species on this planet, whether they support human needs or not. When the early Manhattanites decided to bury Collect Pond, no one mapped out the impact pathways on the ecology of Lower Manhattan. They just thought they would get rid of an increasingly polluted lake and build some new houses.

Skeptics will argue that, yes, there are some environmental planners out there who are concerned with wetlands wildlife, but if you look at the planet as a whole, we are trashing it at an unprecedented clip. The last two centuries have clearly been the most environmentally destructive of any in human history: for every fish we preserved in Meadow Lake, there are a thousand species we have driven to extinction. Isn't this clear evidence that we are making worse choices in the modern age?

But the truth is, on a species level, we have been as destructive ecologically as our technology would allow for at least twenty thousand years, maybe longer. No doubt there were some preindustrial communities who factored the "balance of nature" into their collective decisions about what to eat and where to live. But for most of human history, we have been willing to sacrifice just about any natural resource if it aided our short-term needs. Consider the list of mammals driven into extinction during the first few thousand years that humans occupied North America, from roughly 11,000 to 8000 BC: mastodons, jaguars, woolly mammoths, saber-toothed cats, and at least a dozen other species of bears, antelopes, horses, and other animals. For most of our history, our carnage has been reined in far more by our technological limitations than by our intellectual or moral ones. We've always churned through everything our tools have allowed us to. We just have better tools now—if "better" is the right word for it—so we can do more damage.

The fish in Meadow Lake, on the other hand, suggest a new kind of deliberation: the decision to preserve a species even if it provides little value to us, in the short term, at least. People have been burying the pond since the Stone Age gave them tools to dig with. But contemplating the impact of nitrogen runoff on an algae bloom and how that bloom might starve the fish of oxygen—that is a new way of thinking.

The fact that some of us continue to debate whether global warming is even happening—let alone what we should do about it—shows us that we're still not experts at this kind of thinking. Yes, it does seem ominous that the United States is currently threatening to withdraw from the Paris climate accord. But we are very early in that particular narrative; the ending is not at all clear. So far, the Paris Agreement story is really the story of two distinct decisions: 198 nations signing the accord itself, and one temperamental leader promising to withdraw in a huff. Approached from the long view, which one looks more impressive? We've had impetuous leaders since the birth of agriculture; truly global accords with real consequences for everyday life are a new concoction.

The fact that we sometimes seem incompetent at these kinds of choices is a sign that we are grading on a reverse curve: we have higher standards now, so it sometimes seems as though we're less deliberative than our ancestors. But the truth is, both the spectrum of our decisions and their time horizons have widened dramatically over the past few centuries. The Aztecs and the Greeks could peer into the future as far as their calendars and their crude astronomy would allow them. They built institutions and structures designed explicitly to last centuries. But they never contemplated decisions that addressed problems that wouldn't arrive for another fifty years. They could see cycles and continuity on the long scale. But they couldn't anticipate emergent problems.

We are better predictors of the future, and our decisions are beginning to reflect that new ability. The problem is that the future is coming at us faster than ever before.

THE LONG VIEW

How long could our time horizons be extended? As individuals, almost all of us will find ourselves contemplating at least a few decisions that by definition extend the length of our lives: who to marry, whether to have children, where to live, what vocation to pursue. As a society we are actively deliberating decisions with time horizons that extend beyond a century, in climate change, automation and artificial intelligence, medicine, and urban planning. Could the horizon recede even farther?

Consider a decision that most of us probably do not, initially, at least, have strong feelings about either way: Should we talk to intelligent life-forms living on other planets? In 2015, a dozen or so science and tech luminaries, including Elon Musk, signed a statement that answered that question with a vehement no: "Intentionally signaling other civilizations in the Milky Way Galaxy," the statement argued, "raises concerns from all the people of Earth, about both the message and the consequences of contact. A worldwide scientific, political and humanitarian discussion must occur before any message is sent." They argued, in effect, that an advanced alien civilization might respond to our interstellar greetings with the same graciousness that Cortés showed the Aztecs. The statement was a response to a growing movement led by a multidisciplinary group of astronomers, psychologists, anthropologists, and amateur space enthusiasts that aims to send messages specifically targeting planets in the Milky Way that are likely to support life. Instead of just scanning the skies for signs of intelligent life, the way SETI's telescopes do, this new approach, sometimes called METI (Messaging Extraterrestrial Intelligence), actively tries to initiate contact. The METI organization, led by former SETI scientist Douglas Vakoch, has planned a series of messages to be broadcast from 2018 onward. And Yuri Milner's Breakthrough Listen endeavor has also promised to support a "Breakthrough Message" companion project, including an open competition to design the messages to be transmitted to the stars. Think of it as a kind of intergalactic design charrette.

If you believe that the message has a plausible chance of making contact with an alien intelligence, it's hard not to think of it as one of the most important decisions we will ever make as a species. Are we going to be galactic introverts, huddled behind the door listening for signs of life outside? Or are we going to be extroverted conversation starters? (And if it's the latter, what should we say?) The decision to send a message into space may not generate a meaningful outcome for a thousand years, or even a hundred thousand years, given the transit times between the correspondents. The first intentional message ever sent—the famous Arecibo Message sent by Frank Drake in the 1970s—was addressing a cluster of stars fifty thousand light-years away. The laws of physics dictate the minimum time for the result of that decision to become perceptible to us: one hundred thousand years. It is hard to imagine a decision confronting humanity with a longer leash on the future.

The anti-METI movement is predicated on the fact that if we do ever manage to make contact with another intelligent lifeform, almost by definition our new pen pals will be far more advanced than we are. (A less advanced civilization would be incapable of detecting our signal, and it would be a staggering coincidence if we happened to make contact with a civilization that was at the same level of technological sophistication as ours.) It is this asymmetry that has convinced so many future-minded thinkers that METI is a bad idea. The human history of exploitation weighs heavily on the imagination of the METI critics. Stephen Hawking, for instance, announced in a 2010 documentary series, "If aliens visit us, the outcome would be much as when Columbus landed in America, which didn't turn out well for the Native Americans." Astronomer and sci-fi author David Brin echoes the Hawking critique: "*Every single case* we know of a more technologically advanced culture contacting a less technologically advanced culture resulted at least in pain."

There is something about the METI decision that forces the mind to stretch beyond its usual limits. Using your own human intelligence, you have to imagine some radically different form of intelligence. You have to imagine time scales where a decision made in 2017 might trigger momentous consequences ten thousand years from now. The sheer magnitude of those consequences challenges our usual measures of cause and effect. If you think METI has a reasonable chance of making contact with another intelligent organism somewhere in the Milky Way, then you have to accept that this small group of astronomers and science-fiction authors and billionaire patrons may, in fact, be wrestling with a decision that could prove to be the most transformative one in the history of human civilization.

All of which takes us back to a much more down-to-earth but no less challenging question: *Who gets to decide?* After many years of debate, the SETI community established an agreed-upon procedure that scientists and government agencies should follow in the event that SETI actually stumbles upon an intelligible signal from space. The protocols specifically ordain that "no response to a signal or other evidence of extraterrestrial intelligence should be sent until appropriate international consultations have taken place." But an equivalent set of guidelines does not yet exist to govern our own interstellar outreach.

The METI debate runs parallel to other existential decisions that we will be confronting in the coming decades, as our technological and scientific powers increase. Should we create superintelligent machines that exceed our own intellectual capabilities by such a wide margin that we cease to understand how their intelligence works? Should we "cure" death, as many Silicon Valley visionaries are proposing? Like METI, these are potentially among the most momentous decisions human beings will ever make, and yet the number of people actively participating in that decision—so far—is minuscule.

One of the most thoughtful participants in the debate over the METI decision, Kathryn Denning, an anthropologist at York University in Toronto, has argued that decisions like METI require a far wider sample of stakeholders: "I think the METI debate may be one of those rare topics where scientific knowledge is highly relevant to the discussion, but its connection to obvious policy is tenuous at best, because in the final analysis, it's all about how much risk the people of Earth are willing to tolerate . . . and why exactly should astronomers, cosmologists, physicists, anthropologists, psychologists, sociologists, biologists, scifi authors, or anyone else (in no particular order) get to decide what those tolerances should be?"

Agreements like SETI protocols—and even the Paris climate accord—should be seen as genuine achievements in the history of human decision-making. But they are closer to norms than to actual legislation. They do not have the force of law behind them. Norms are powerful things. But as we have seen in recent years, norms can also be fragile, easily undermined by disrupters who don't mind offending the mainstream. And they are rarely strong enough to resist the march of technological innovation.

The fragility of norms may be most apparent in decisions that involve extinction-level risk. New technologies (like self-replicating machines) or interventions (like METI) that pose even the slightest risk to our survival as a species require much more global oversight. Creating those regulations would force us to, as Denning suggests, measure risk tolerance on a planetary level. They would require a kind of global Bad Events Table, only instead of calculating the risk magnitude of events that would unfold in a matter of seconds, as the Google algorithm does, the table would measure risk for events that might not emerge for centuries. If we don't build institutions that can measure that risk tolerance, then by default the gamblers will always set the agenda, and the rest of us will have to live with the consequences. This same pattern applies to choices that aren't as much about existential risk as they are about existential *change*. Most Americans and Europeans, when asked, say they would not like to "cure" death; they say they much prefer pursuing longer, more meaningful lives, not immortality. But if immortality is, in fact, within our reach technologically—and there is at least some persuasive evidence to suggest it is—we don't necessarily have the institutions in place that are equipped to stop it. Do we want to have the option to live forever? That is a global, species-level decision if there ever was one.

How would we go about making decisions like this? We do have institutions like the United Nations that gave us a framework for making planetary choices, and for all the limitations of its power, the fact that the UN exists at all is a measure of real progress. If our decision-making prowess improves with the growing diversity of the group making the decision, it's hard to imagine a more farsighted institution than one that represents all the countries of the world. But, of course, the United Nations represents the citizens of those countries through very indirect means. Its decisions are hardly direct expressions of the "will of the people." Would it be possible to conduct something equivalent to a design charrette on the scale of the planet, where stakeholders—not just political appointees—can weigh in with their own priorities and tolerance for risk?

We invented the institution of democracy—in all its many guises—to help us decide, as a society, what our laws should be.

Perhaps it is time that we took some of the lessons we have learned from small-group decision-making and applied them to the realm of mass decisions. This is not as unlikely as it sounds. After all, the rise of the Internet has enabled us to reinvent the way we communicate multiple times in my lifetime alone: from email to blogs to Facebook status updates. Why shouldn't we take this opportunity to reinvent our decision-making tools as well?

There is some evidence that Internet crowds can be harnessed to set priorities and suggest options with more acumen than the so-called experts, if the software tools organizing all that collective intelligence (and stupidity) are designed properly. In the month leading up to the 2008 inauguration, the incoming Obama administration opened up a Citizen's Briefing Book on the web, inviting the US population to suggest priorities for the next four years—a small experiment in direct democracy inspired by the Open Government movement that was then on the rise. Ordinary citizens could suggest initiatives and also vote to support other initiatives. In the end, two of the three most popular initiatives urged Obama to radically reform our draconian drug laws and end marijuana prohibition. At the time, the results provoked titters from the media establishment: This is what happens when you open the gates to the Internet crazies; you get a horde of stoners suggesting policy that has zero chance of mainstream support. And yet by the end of Obama's second term, that briefing book turned out to be the first glimmer of an idea whose time had come. Sentencing laws were being rewritten, cannabis was legal in half a dozen states, and a majority of Americans now support full legalization.

In a polarized, nationalistic age, the idea of global oversight on any issue, however existential the threat it poses, may sound naive. And it may well be that technologies have their own inevitability, and we can only rein them in in the short run. Reducing our carbon footprint, by comparison, may prove to be an easier choice than stopping something like METI or immortality research, because there is an increasingly visible path for minimizing climate change that involves adopting even more advanced technology: not retreating back to a preindustrial life, but moving forward into a world of carbon-neutral technology, like solar panels and electric vehicles. In our history, there is not a lot of precedent of human beings voluntarily swearing off a new technological capability—or choosing not to make contact with another society—because of some threat that might not arrive for generations. But maybe it's time we learned how to make that kind of decision.

SUPERINTELLIGENCE

The development of supercomputers like Cheyenne—computers smart enough to map the impact pathways of climate change a hundred years into the future—has endowed us with two kinds of farsightedness: they let us predict future changes in our climate that help us make better decisions about our energy use and our carbon footprint today, and they suggest long-term trends in the development of artificial intelligence, trends that may pose their own existential threat to humans in the coming centuries. The upward trajectory of Moore's law and recent advances in machine learning have convinced many scientists and technologists that we must confront a new global decision: what to do with the potential threat from "superintelligent" machines. If computers reach a level of intelligence where they can outperform humans at nuanced decisions like rendering a verdict in a complicated criminal trial, they will almost certainly have been programmed by evolutionary algorithms, where the code follows a kind of vastly accelerated version of Darwin's natural selection. Humans will program some original base of code, and then the system will experiment with random variations at blistering speed, selecting the variants that improve the intelligence of the machine and mutating that new "species" of code. Run enough cycles and the machine may evolve an intellectual sophistication without any human programmer understanding how the machine got so smart. In recent years, a growing number of scientists and tech-sector leaders—Bill Gates, Elon Musk, Stephen Hawking—have sounded the alarm that a superintelligent AI could pose a potential "existential threat" to humanity.

All of which suggests that we are going to confront a decision as a planet: Are we going to allow superintelligent machines, or not? It's possible that we will "make" the decision in the same way the citizens of New York made the decision to fill Collect Pond, or the way the inventors of the industrial age decided to fill the atmosphere with carbon. In other words, we'll make it in an entirely unstructured, bottom-up way, without any of the long-term deliberation the decision warrants. We'll keep opting for smarter and smarter computers because in the short term, they're better at scheduling meetings and curating workout playlists and driving our cars for us. But those choices won't reflect the potential long-term threat posed by superintelligent machines.

Why would these machines be so dangerous? To understand the threat, you need to shed some of your human biases about the scales of intellectual ability. As AI theorist Eliezer Yudkowsky puts it, we have a "human tendency to think of 'village idiot' and 'Einstein' as the extreme ends of the intelligence scale, instead of nearly indistinguishable points on the scale of minds-in-general." From the point of view of, say, a mouse, the village idiot and Einstein are both unfathomably intelligent. We spent the first decades of AI research mostly dreaming about building machines that might function at a village-idiot level of intelligence or perhaps reach the Einsteinian summit. But as the philosopher Nick Bostrom and Yudowsky both argue, there's no reason to think that the Einsteinian summit is some sort of fundamental upper limit. "Far from being the smartest possible biological species," Bostrom writes, "we are probably better thought of as the stupidest possible biological species capable of starting a technological civilization—a niche we filled because we got there first, not because we are in any sense optimally adapted to it." Powered by recursive, self-learning algorithms, the first true AI might well march right past Mount Einstein and ascend to some higher plateau well beyond our imagining.

The danger perceived by people like Bostrom or Hawking does not look exactly like the standard science-fiction version. First, it is not at all necessary that the AI become conscious (or "self-aware," as the original *Terminator* put it). A superintelligent AI might develop some kind of alternative consciousness, likely completely different from ours. But it also might remain a vast assemblage of insentient calculations, capable of expression and action and long-term planning, but lacking a sense of self. Secondly, the AI need not suddenly turn evil or vengeful or ambitious (or any other anthropomorphic emotion) to destroy human civilization. Bostrom, for instance, spends almost no time in his influential book *Superintelligence* imagining machines becoming evil overlords; instead, he worries about small miscommunications in defining the AI's goals or motivations that could lead to global or even cosmic transformations. Consider programming an AI with as seemingly an innocuous goal as you could imagine: Bentham's "greatest happiness for the greatest number." You set that as the overarching value and let the machine decide the best approach to making it a reality. Maximizing human happiness would seem to be a perfectly laudable objective, but the AI might well come up with a scenario that, while technically achieving the objective, would be immediately abhorrent to humans: perhaps the AI distributes nanobots into every human brain on the planet, permanently stimulating the pleasure centers of the brain and turning us all into grinning zombies. The threat is not that when asked to decide the best strategy for combating some environmental crisis, the AI will actively disobey us and instead hack into the Department of Defense network and detonate its entire nuclear arsenal because it has evolved some inherent evilness or desire for conquest. The threat is that we will ask it to find the optimal solution for an environmental crisis, and it will decide to eliminate the main cause of the crisis—human beings—because we haven't framed the objective clearly enough.

Much of the debate over superintelligent AI is devoted to thinking through what is sometimes called the "containment problem," brilliantly explored in Alex Garland's film *Ex Machina*: how to keep the genie of AI inside the bottle, while still tapping into its powers. Could humans evolve an AI that was truly superintelligent, but at the same time keep it safely bounded so that a runaway instruction doesn't trigger a global catastrophe? In Bostrom's convincing presentation, the problem is much harder than it might first appear, in large part because the humans would be trying to outthink an intelligence that is orders of magnitude more advanced than their own. Containing the AI will be like a mouse scheming to influence human technological advancement to prevent the invention of mousetraps.

In a way, we are at a point in the conversation about superintelligence equivalent to where the global warming debate was in the late 1980s: a small group of scientists and researchers and public intellectuals extrapolating out from current trends and predicting a major crisis looming several generations down the line. According to a survey conducted by Bostrom, most of the AI research community believes superhuman-level AI is still at least fifty years away.

That multigenerational time scale may be the most encouraging element in a debate filled with doomsday scenarios. Climate advocates often complain about the sluggish pace of political and corporate reform given the magnitude of the global warming threat. But we should remind ourselves that with climate change, we are trying to make a series of decisions that are arguably without precedent in human history: deciding which regulatory and technological interventions to put in place to prevent a threat that may not have a severe impact on most humans for several decades, if not longer. For all the biases and intuitive leaps of System 1, one of the hallmarks of human intelligence is the long-term decision-making of System 2: our ability to make short-term sacrifices in the service of more distant goals, the planning and forward thinking of *Homo prospectus*. While we are not flawless at it by any means, we are better at that kind of thinking than any other species on the planet. But we have never used those decision-making skills to wrestle with a problem that doesn't exist yet, a problem we anticipate arising in the distant future based on our examination of current trends.

To be clear, humans have made decisions to engineer many ingenious projects with the explicit aim of ensuring that they last for centuries: pyramids, dynasties, monuments, democracies. Some infrastructure decisions—like the dike system of the Netherlands or Japanese building codes designed to protect against tsunamis—anticipate threats that might not happen for a century or more, though those threats are not genuinely new ones: those cultures know to be concerned about floods and tsunamis because they have experienced them in the past. Some decisions that we have made, like the decision to adopt democratic governance, have been explicitly designed to solve as-of-yet-undiscovered problems by engineering resilience and flexibility into their codes and conventions. But mostly those exercises in long-term planning have been all about preserving the current order, not making a preemptive choice to protect us against threats that might erupt three generations later. In a way, the closest analogues to the current interventions on climate (and the growing AI discussion) are eschatological: in religious traditions that encourage us to make present-day decisions based on an anticipated Judgment Day that may not arrive for decades, or millennia.

With superintelligence, as with climate change, we are trying something new as a species. We are actively thinking about the choices we are making *now* in order to achieve a better outcome fifty years from now. But superintelligence is an even more ambitious undertaking, because the problem we are anticipating is qualitatively different from today's reality. Climate change forces us to imagine a world that is a few degrees hotter than our current situation, with longer droughts, more intense storms, and so on. We talk about global warming "destroying the planet," but that language is hyperbole: the planet will be fine even if we do nothing to combat global warming. Even in the worst-case scenario, *Homo sapiens* as a species would survive a five-degree increase in surface temperatures—though not without immense suffering and mortality. A truly superintelligent machine—capable, for example, of building self-replicating nano-machines that devour all carbon-based life—could plausibly pose an extinction-level threat to us. But there is nothing in our current landscape or our history that resembles this kind of threat. We have to imagine it.

Interestingly, one of the key tools we have had in training our minds to make this momentous choice has been storytelling—science fiction, to be precise, which turns out to play a role in some of our mass decisions equivalent to the role scenario planning plays in our group decisions. "This kind of exercise is generally new," the writer and futurist Kevin Kelly suggests, "because we all now accept that the world of our grandchildren will be markedly different than our world—which was not true before. I believe this is the function of science fiction. To parse, debate, rehearse, question, and prepare us for the future of new. For at least a century, science fiction has served to anticipate the future . . . In the past there have been many laws prohibiting new inventions as they appeared. But I am unaware of any that prohibited inventions before they appeared. I read this as a cultural shift from science fiction as entertainment to science fiction as infrastructure—a necessary method of anticipation." Science-fiction narratives have been ruminating on the pitfalls of artificial intelligence for at least a century—from the "global brain" of H. G. Wells to HAL 9000 all the way to *Ex Machina*—but only in the last few years has the problem entered into real-world conversation and debate. The novels primed us to see the problem more clearly, helped us peer around the limits of our technology-bounded rationality. No doubt the superintelligent machines will climb their way past human intelligence by running ensemble simulations at unimaginable speeds, but if we manage to keep them from destroying life as we know it, it will be, in part, because the much slower simulations of novels helped us understand the threat more clearly.

Given the accelerating rates of change of modern society, the current debate about AI and its potential threats is a bit like a group of inventors and scientists gathering together in the early 1800s and saying, "This industrial revolution is certainly going to make us much more productive, and in the long run raise standards of living, but we also appear to be pumping a lot of carbon into the atmosphere, which will likely come back to haunt us in a couple of centuries, so we should think about how to prevent that problem." But, of course, that conversation didn't happen, because we didn't have the tools to measure the carbon in the air, or computer simulations to help us predict how that carbon would influence temperatures globally, or a history of battling other industrial pollutants, or government and academic institutions that monitor climate and ecosystem change, or sci-fi novels that imagined a scenario where new technologies somehow altered global weather patterns. We were smart enough to invent coal-powered engines, but not yet smart enough to predict their ultimate impact on the environment.

The AI debate is yet another reminder of how much progress we have made in our ability to make farsighted decisions. All those tools and sensors and narratives that have enabled us to identify the threat of climate change or imagine an AI apocalypse constitute, en masse, their own kind of superintelligence.

"We are as gods," Stewart Brand famously wrote a half century ago. "We might as well get good at it." We have indeed developed godlike powers over our planet's atmosphere in just under three hundred years of carbon-based industry. Are we good at it yet, though? Probably not. But we're quick learners. And we're certainly taking on global decisions with time horizons that our immediate ancestors would have found astonishing. The fact that challenges are still emerging to long-term global decisions like the Paris Agreement is inevitable: it's hard enough to project forward fifty years as an individual, much less as a society. But just the existence of these debates—AI, climate change, METI—make it clear that we are beginning to explore a new kind of farsightedness. With AI, all the projections of future threats may well turn out to be false alarms, either because true AI turns out to be far more difficult to achieve, or because we discover new techniques that minimize the danger before the machines march on past Mount Einstein. But if artificial superintelligence does turn out to pose an existential threat, our best defense will likely come out of our own new powers of *human* superintelligence: mapping, predicting, simulating, taking the long view.

THE DRAKE EQUATION

Superintelligence, climate change, and METI share another property beyond their extended time horizons. They are all decisions that cannot be properly appraised without the consultation of a wide range of intellectual disciplines. Climate science alone is a hybrid of multiple fields: molecular chemistry, atmospheric science, fluid dynamics, thermodynamics, hydrology, computer science, ecology, and many more. Defining the problem of climate change didn't just require the digital simulations of Cheyenne; it also required a truly heroic collaboration between disciplines. But deciding what to do about climate change requires a whole other set of fields as well: political science, economics, industrial history, and behavioral psychology, for instance. The problem of superintelligence draws on expertise in artificial intelligence, evolution, and software design, but it also has been profoundly illuminated by philosophical inquiries and the imagined futures of science fiction. Some amount of intellectual diversity is required in any full-spectrum decision, of course; even the most intimate choice, as we will see in the next chapter, draws on multiple bands of experience to settle on an optimal path. But these mass decisions—the ones that may well involve existential risk to us as a species—require an even wider slice of the spectrum.

A little more than a decade before he transmitted his famous Arecibo Message—the one that cannot, by definition, receive a reply for another hundred thousand years—Frank Drake sketched out one of the great equations in modern scientific history, as a way of framing the decision of whether to seek contact with lifeforms on other planets. If we start scanning the cosmos for signs of intelligent life, Drake asked, how likely are we to actually detect something? The equation didn't generate a clear answer; it was more of an attempt to build a full-spectrum map of all the relevant variables. In mathematical form, the Drake equation looks like this:

$$N = R_* \times f_p \times n_e \times f_l \times f_i \times f_c \times L$$

N represents the number of extant, communicative civilizations in the Milky Way. The initial variable R_* corresponds to the rate of star formation in the galaxy, effectively giving you the total number of potential suns that could support life. The remaining variables then serve as a kind of nested sequence of filters: Given the number of stars in the Milky Way, what fraction of those have planets, and how many of those have an environment that can support life? On those potentially hospitable planets, how often does life itself actually emerge, and what fraction of that life evolves into intelligent life, and what fraction of that life eventually leads to a civilization's transmitting detectable signals into space? At the end of his equation, Drake placed the crucial variable L, which is the average length of time during which those civilizations emit those signals.

I know of no other equation that so elegantly conjoins so many different intellectual disciplines in a single framework. As you move from left to right in the equation, you shift from astrophysics, to the biochemistry of life, to evolutionary theory, to cognitive science, all the way to theories of technological development. Your guess about each value in the Drake Equation winds up revealing a whole worldview. Perhaps you think life is rare, but when it does emerge, intelligent life usually follows; or perhaps you think microbial life is ubiquitous throughout the cosmos, but more complex organisms almost never form. The equation is notoriously vulnerable to very different outcomes, depending on the numbers you assign to each variable.

The most provocative value is the last one: L, the average life span of a signal-transmitting civilization. You don't have to be a Pollyanna to defend a relatively high L value. You just have to believe it's possible for civilizations to become fundamentally self-sustaining and survive for millions of years. Even if one in a thousand intelligent life-forms in space generates a million-year civilization, the value of L increases meaningfully. But if your L value is low, that implies a further question: What is keeping it low? Do technological civilizations keep flickering on and off in the Milky Way, like so many fireflies in space? Do they run out of resources? Do they blow themselves up?

Since Drake first sketched out the equation in 1961, two fundamental developments have reshaped our understanding of the problem. First, the product of the first three values in the equation (representing our best guess at the number of stars with habitable planets) has increased by several orders of magnitude. And second, we have been listening for signals for decades and heard nothing. If the habitable planet value keeps getting bigger and bigger without any sign of intelligent life in our scans, the question becomes: Which of the other variables are the filters? Perhaps life itself is astonishingly rare, even on habitable planets. From our perspective, as human beings living in the first decades of the third millennium, wondering whether we are flirting with existential risks through our technological hubris, we want the emergence of intelligent life to be astonishingly rare; if the opposite is true, and intelligent life is abundant in the Milky Way, then L values might be low, perhaps measured in centuries and not even millennia. In that case, the adoption of a technologically advanced lifestyle might be effectively simultaneous with extinction. First you invent radio, then you invent technologies capable of destroying all life on your planet and shortly thereafter you push the button and your civilization goes dark.

Perhaps this is the ironic fate of any species that achieves the farsightedness of *Homo prospectus*. Perhaps every time a species on some Earth-like planet evolves a form of intelligence smart enough to imagine alternate futures, smart enough to turn those imaginative acts into reality, that cognitive leap forward sets off a chain reaction of technological escalation that ultimately deprives that species of its actual future. The early silence that has greeted our SETI probes so far suggests that this is at the very least a possibility. But perhaps that escalation is an arms race that is not doomed to end in apocalypse. Maybe the L values are high, and the universe is teeming with intelligent life that made it through the eye of the needle of industrialization without catastrophe. Maybe it's possible to invent ways of making farsighted choices as a society faster than we invent new ways of destroying ourselves. Certainly it's essential for us to try. If those superintelligent machines do manage to assist human civilization, and not accidentally trigger the mass extinction that Bostrom and Hawking fear, it will be because those machines learned how to make decisions that assessed the full spectrum of variables and consequences, that ran ensemble simulations that allowed them to tease out all the unanticipated consequences and discover new options. Perhaps the machines will evolve that farsightedness on their own, through some kind of self-learning algorithm. But wouldn't it be better if we were wise enough by then to give them a head start?

5

THE PERSONAL CHOICE

Her world was in a state of convulsive change; the only
thing she could say distinctly to herself was, that she
must wait and think anew.

• GEORGE ELIOT, *MIDDLEMARCH*

I am ready to sit down and weep at the impossibility of
my understanding or barely knowing even a fraction of
the sum of objects that present themselves for our
contemplation in books and in life. Have I then any
time to spend on things that never existed?

• FROM THE DIARY OF SIXTEEN-YEAR-OLD
MARY ANN EVANS

Sometime in January 1851, Darwin pulled out the notebook where he had been recording his water cure treatments, opened it to a new page, and scrawled out a
headline: "Annie." After years of being the member of his household with the most health complaints, Darwin now found himself shifting his role from patient to physician, tending this time
to Annie, his beloved ten-year-old daughter. Annie and her sis-
ters had suffered from scarlet fever in 1849, and while the other
two girls had made a full recovery, Annie remained frail in the
months that followed. In late 1850 she came down with a severe

fever and began vomiting. ("She inherits I fear with grief my wretched indigestion," Darwin wrote in his diary.) Dr. Gully at the Malvern spa was consulted, and the Darwins began applying a home version of the water cure to their daughter, with Charles recording the results in his notebook daily.

By March 1851, Annie's health had deteriorated to the point where a more dramatic intervention seemed necessary, and so the Darwins made the fateful decision to send their daughter to Malvern to be treated directly by Dr. Gully. Darwin accompanied her and wrote back regular dispatches to Emma, who was then in the third trimester of a pregnancy. Gully's treatments ranged from useless (a poultice of mustard was regularly applied to her stomach) to downright toxic (she was prescribed a "medicine" of camphor and ammonia, the latter a deadly poison). More troublingly, she developed symptoms that resembled those of typhoid, suggesting perhaps that the constant immersion in water at Malvern may not have been as sanitary as Gully claimed. When she finally died on April 23, Gully wrote an evasive cause of death on the death certificate: "bilious fever with typhoid character."

Annie's death would prove to be the great tragedy of Darwin's life. "She went to her final sleep most tranquilly, most sweetly at 12 oclock today," he wrote Emma from Malvern. "Our poor dear child has had a very short life but I trust happy. I cannot remember ever seeing the dear child naughty. God bless her. We must be more & more to each other my dear wife." Later, in his journals, he wrote, "We have lost the joy of the household, and the solace of our old age. Oh that she could now know how deeply, how tenderly we do still & shall ever love her dear joyous face."

Her death turned Darwin from a religious skeptic into a hardened nonbeliever. "The doctrines of the Bible that Emma took comfort in were hurdles he could not jump," his biographer Janet Browne writes, "not even with an overwhelming desire to believe in an afterlife for Anne." He stopped attending formal church services, choosing instead to accompany Emma and the children to the local chapel's front door on Sunday morning and then walk through the neighborhood during the service.

But if Annie's death intensified Darwin's nonbelief, it added a devastating new complication to the decision he had been wrestling with for more than a decade: whether to publish his radical theory of evolution. The concept of natural selection had always had a mercurial power over Darwin. From the very beginning, he was torn between the desire to sing it from the rooftops and the desire to keep it locked away in a drawer. But Annie's death pulled him in even more directions, with greater force. Having spent more than a decade exploring the parameters of his theory— writing down all the objections he could come up with and, one by one, knocking them down—Darwin was even more convinced that he was sitting on one of the most important ideas of the century, if not the millennium. That made him eager to share it, both because it was true and because he would invariably be recognized for the achievement. He was driven by both a superhuman drive to understand the world and an all-too-human desire for vindication.

But he was also driven by his attachment to Emma and his children, not to mention the memory of Annie. This was the double edge of meaning in the whole notion of being "recognized" for your work. He would become *the* Darwin, the one with the dangerous idea. It was not implausible that he would receive some kind of formal denunciation from the church. The gulf in religious belief that had always separated Charles and Emma grew even wider and more turbulent after Annie's death. Faith in salvation and the afterlife kept Emma afloat in the wake of losing her child. Releasing his heretical ideas into the world would have been the equivalent of Darwin putting stones in Emma's pockets. He might have been ready to suffer the public shame of condemnation, but he was not ready to suffer the private guilt of challenging his grieving wife's faith.

It is hard to imagine a decision that spanned such a wide spectrum, from the most intimate feelings of love and loss shared with your spouse all the way out to the tectonic shifts of a society's religious beliefs. Sketching out the impact pathways alone required a vast canvas. Natural selection happened to be one of those rare ideas that reverberate for centuries. Amplified by Darwin's later argument for a common ancestor shared by humans and apes, it would deliver the most empirical of the three Victorian-era renunciations of God that made nonbelief part of the mainstream of popular opinion. Marx made the political case. Nietzsche made the philosophical case. But Darwin did it with *evidence*.

I think it's fair to say that most of us will never face a decision of that magnitude. And so we can probably forgive Darwin that he never actually managed to make the decision. He opted to stall, until Alfred Russel Wallace threatened—in the most civil way possible—to publish his own independent discovery of the principles that Darwin had been privately mulling for two decades. The decision that Darwin had considered up until that point was not hard because the forecast was murky. Darwin had the predictive part right: evolution would change everything. It was hard because the deep values at stake were fundamentally irreconcilable. There was no third way to release evolution into the wild and *not* challenge the doctrines of Christianity, not announce to the world that your wife's solace was nothing more than a myth.

Or perhaps, in a semiconscious way, Darwin did figure out a third option: to stay in a state of suspended distraction—researching his barnacles and pigeons, and revising his drafts—until someone forced his hand. By the time he finally published *On the Origin of Species*, Emma had long reconciled herself to her husband's lack of faith, and he could hardly be blamed for wanting to put his theory into circulation under his own name first.

What I find so arresting—and tragic—about Darwin's decision is that it somehow managed to be both achingly intimate and immensely public at the same time. Its downstream ripples shaped both the love and faith of his wife *and* our collective understanding of humanity's place in the universe. And yet for all the scope of it, the decision was not one that could be made by a charrette or a democratic vote or a jury; it was a decision that largely had to be adjudicated in Darwin's own mind, with the help of his wife and closest friends. And while it is true that very few of us will ever confront a decision with such a wide spectrum of consequences, it is also true that most of the important personal decisions we make in our lives do require some kind of full-spectrum deliberation. Their half-life may be measured in years or decades—and not centuries, as in Darwin's choice, or the choice to bury Collect Pond—but they share the same fundamental challenges that exist in many of the decisions we have explored over the preceding chapters: how to take a complex, multivariable situation shaped by many "threadlike pressures" and chart a path into the future.

GO WEST, MIDDLE-AGED MAN

This book itself dates back to a personal decision in my own life, one that is still reverberating as I write, seven years after I first started wrestling with it. At some point in the winter of 2011, as I was climbing over the three feet of snow that stayed piled on our Brooklyn sidewalk from late December to February, it occurred to me that it was time to move to California. I had lived half my life in New York: spent my grad school years up in Morningside Heights; moved in with my wife and had our first child in the West Village; and then, like so many of my New York friends, moved to Brooklyn when our second son was on the way. It was a thrilling two decades, but as I grew older, each February my internal arguments for California would roll in, as predictable as the frigid weather itself, and then retreat with the arrival of spring. But eventually they dropped anchor.

I spent a lot of time justifying the move to myself before I even floated the idea to my wife. Our children were the perfect age for the adventure, I told myself: old enough to appreciate it, but not so old that they would refuse to make the move because they couldn't bear to leave their pals behind. To not take advantage of that opportunity, even for a few years, seemed like a terrible waste. And as much as I still loved New York, and especially

Brooklyn, there were things to love about California, too, particularly the Bay Area—its epic natural beauty, its long history as
a driver of cultural change and new ideas.

There was a philosophical argument for the move as well: I
had come to think that this kind of change was intrinsically
good, wherever you happened to move. An old friend who had
done a similar westward migration a few years before told me
that the great thing about moving is that the changed context
helps you understand yourself and your family more deeply: you
get to see all the things that you really loved about your old
home—and the things that always bothered you without you
fully recognizing it. Like a good control study in a science experiment, the contrast allowed you to see what really mattered.
Changing the background scenery helped you see the foreground
more clearly.

And then there was the passage of time. Another old friend—
who had been in New York with me for two decades, both of us
watching our kids grow up at lightning speed—sent me an email
weighing in on the decision to move west. "Change like this
slows down time," he wrote. When you're in your routine, fre-
quenting the same old haunts, time seems to accelerate—was it
just four years ago that our youngest son was born? But all the
complexities of moving—figuring out where to live, getting
there, and then navigating all the new realities of the changed
environment—means that the minutes and hours that once passed
as a kind of background process, the rote memory of knowing
your place, are suddenly thrust into your conscious awareness.
You have to figure it out, and figuring things out makes you
more acutely aware of the passing days and months. You get

disoriented, or at least you have to think for a while before you can be properly oriented again.

So that was why we should move, I preached to my own internal choir: for the positive effect it would have on our kids, the natural beauty, the climate, the Bay Area tech scene, the many friends out there who I hadn't seen enough of over the past twenty years. And on top of all that, the move would help us slow down time.

I felt, to be honest, as though I had built a fairly solid— perhaps even poetic—case for the move. Beyond the simple demography of the move itself—five new residents added to the California state population tally, and five deducted from the New York rolls—it was not a public decision at all. And yet even my initial list of arguments in favor of the move took up a lot of the spectrum. The cost-benefit analysis was a multilayered one, even if I mostly saw benefits. Deciding to move to California was partly an economic decision about the cost of living in a city versus a suburb, but it also raised psychological questions about how important the presence of nature is to your life and the lives of your children. For me, it was also a decision about the arc I wanted for my life: Was I going to be the kind of person who lived in one place for most of his adult life, or was I going to be someone who spent meaningful amounts of time in different places? There were other more quantifiable factors to consider as well: the schools, the weather, the practical implications of selling our place in Brooklyn.

Darwin had his private pros-vs.-cons list. I turned my argument, embarrassingly enough, into a PowerPoint deck, sat my wife down in front of my computer one snowy day in February, and walked her through the reasons. Later, I turned to writing letters, three or four pages single-spaced, walking through the logic as I saw it at the time.

But as comprehensive as I thought my map was, my wife's response to the initial argument made me realize that I had only begun to inventory all the threads. Her map was both more social and more political. We had many friends in our neighborhood in Brooklyn whom we'd known for twenty years or more; how severe was the cost of losing our day-to-day connection to those people, and giving up the whole "it takes a village" experience of raising kids with a tight-knit group of old friends who live within walking distance? And what did it mean to give up the pedestrian density of Brooklyn for the car-centric lifestyle of suburban California?

We tugged back and forth at the problem for a few months, and ultimately found an undiscovered path, another option that took the decision beyond the simple "whether or not" choice that I had originally proposed: We decided to move to California for two years, but also agreed that after that experiment, if my wife wanted to return to Brooklyn, we would move back, no questions asked. It seemed like a good idea at the time, and with the hindsight of seven years I think both my wife and I would agree that it was. But the actual experience of moving was, hands down, the most traumatic episode in our marriage. We dropped down into a neighborhood where my wife knew almost no one; she felt tragically disconnected from her friends back east. I ended up having to travel to promote a new book for the first few months after we arrived, and so every time I crawled off a plane, the beauty of the Bay Area seemed like an impossible refuge, a new life. The gap between our perspectives was immense. She was miserable; I was liberated.

Over time, the gap narrowed. She learned to appreciate the Bay Area's many charms; I began to miss the friends I'd left behind in New York and the ambulatory pleasures of a sidewalk city. We eventually hit upon an additional option that we'd barely considered when I first proposed the move: that we would try to carve out a life on both coasts, spending part of our time in Brooklyn and part in California. But I have often looked back at that decision and wondered if we could have approached it in a way that would have done a better job of reconciling our different values from the beginning. Of course, some of the specific practices we have explored might seem a little comical when used in confronting a personal decision. Conducting a multidisciplinary charrette, for instance, or designing a war game to simulate your move to California probably wouldn't make the choice any clearer. But the general principles of seeking out diverse perspectives on the choice, challenging your assumptions, making an explicit effort to map the variables—all these techniques would almost certainly help you make a more informed decision, and would certainly be a step up from the moral algebra of Ben Franklin's pros-vs.-cons list.

But the science on these kinds of personal choices is necessarily murky. We know a great deal about deliberative group decisions because we have run multiple simulations in the form of controlled experiments with mock juries and war games and fictitious crime investigations. But it is much harder to simulate an intimate decision in a lab experiment—whether it involves moving to California or getting married or any of the other personal choices that define the path of our private lives. For those kinds of decisions, we can learn instead from a different kind of simulation.

DOROTHEA'S CHOICE

Sometime right around when I first began making the argument for the California move, shortly after I turned forty, I began reading novels again. I had gone to grad school to study English lit, so I had spent most of my twenties poring—and, truth be told, sometimes laboring—over the triple-decker narratives of Eliot, Dickens, Balzac, and Zola. But in my mid-twenties I had developed a late-blooming interest in the history of science, so I spent a decade or so catching up, reading almost exclusively nonfiction. But turning forty changed all that: I found myself needing the companionship of novels. Something about beginning to see the longer arc of my life made that kind of narrative increasingly important to me. And one of the first novels I returned to was the one that had made the most vivid impression on me in my twenties: *Middlemarch*.

Middlemarch is many things to many readers, but when reading it in my early forties—as I was contemplating a major decision in my own life—it became clear to me, in a way that had eluded me in my twenties, that the novel offered a remarkably vivid and nuanced portrait of the deciding mind at work. I didn't have the metaphor yet, but what I was responding to then was Eliot's capacity for full-spectrum mapping, showing the many scales of experience that are activated by a complex decision, even one that largely revolves around private concerns. Think of the buzzing intensity of the interior monologue as the high end of the spectrum; the shifting alliances of friends and extended family and town gossip as the midrange; and the slow, sometimes invisible churn of technological or moral history as the low end of the spectrum. Some novels thrive in the narrowband. They home in on the interior monologue or the public sphere. But some novels are full spectrum. They show how those private moments of emotional intensity are inevitably linked to a broader political context; how technological changes rippling through society can impact a marriage; how the chattering of small-town gossip can weigh on one's personal finances. That full-spectrum analysis can make for compelling art, as it does in *Middlemarch*, but it also serves a more instructive purpose, because the complex decisions that we confront in our own lives are almost by definition full-spectrum affairs.

We have already seen some of this portraiture in the *Middlemarch* scene relaying Lydgate's frustration at the threadlike pressures shaping his decision to replace the town vicar. But the decision at the center of *Middlemarch* belongs to its heroine, Dorothea Brooke. It is worth mapping out the full spectrum of Dorothea's choice to demonstrate just how subtle and far-reaching Eliot's account of the decision truly is. But you could substitute any number of other literary decisions, some of them heroic, some tragic, for this one: Lucien Chardon's fateful decision to forge his brother-in-law's signature on three promissory notes near the end of Balzac's *Lost Illusions*; the Lambert family agonizing over what to do with their increasingly senile patriarch in Jonathan Franzen's *The Corrections*. Other narrative forms can also shine light on full-spectrum decision-making: think of Michael Corleone's choice to murder his brother in *The Godfather: Part II*, or Walter White's ultimate endgame in the final season of *Breaking Bad*. All these narratives have compelling plot twists and vividly rendered characters, but what makes them so striking for our purposes is how accurately they map the multidimensional forces that come to bear on the choice itself. To immerse oneself in these stories is, in a sense, to practice the kind of mapping exercises we require in our own lives.

In the first chapters of *Middlemarch*, Dorothea makes a staggering mistake, marrying a dour and aging classical scholar named Edward Casaubon, inspired not by any romantic passion for Casaubon himself, but rather by the idea of a grand intellectual collaboration, assisting with his epic quest to discover the "key to all mythologies." (Dorothea's youthful earnestness appears to have been based on Eliot's own temperament as a young adult.) Casaubon turns out to be one of literature's great duds: as aloof and austere as his marital relations are, his professional work as a scholar proves even more disappointing to Dorothea. She quickly comes to see his grand project as a kind of endless maze, a labyrinth of classical allusions with no underlying pattern to make sense of it all. On their honeymoon in Rome, as her newly-wed buoyancy begins to deflate, she meets a young political reformer named Will Ladislaw, a cousin of Casaubon's with no financial prospects thanks to his mother's scandalous marriage to a Polish musician. Ladislaw and Dorothea develop a platonic but intense friendship, as Ladislaw's energy and political ambitions offer a welcome contrast to the intellectual mausoleum of her married life, which only grows more dismal on returning to Casaubon's large estate in Middlemarch, Lowick Manor. Detecting—correctly, as it happens—the seedlings of a great passion, Casaubon spitefully adds a secret codicil to his will specifically dictating that Dorothea should forfeit his entire estate if she ever marries Will Ladislaw after Casaubon's death.

By Book Five of *Middlemarch*—memorably titled "The Dead Hand"—Casaubon has succumbed to a heart condition, and Dorothea learns for the first time of the provision that her late husband has inserted in his will. Eliot takes us inside Dorothea's shifting consciousness as the news sinks in:

> *She might have compared her experience at that moment to the vague, alarmed consciousness that her life was taking on a new form that she was undergoing a metamorphosis in which memory would not adjust itself to the stirring of new organs. Everything was changing its aspect: her husband's conduct, her own duteous feeling towards him, every struggle between them—and yet more, her whole relation to Will Ladislaw. Her world was in a state of convulsive change; the only thing she could say distinctly to herself was, that she must wait and think anew. One change terrified her as if it had been a sin; it was a violent shock of repulsion from her departed husband, who had had hidden thoughts, perhaps perverting everything she said and did. Then again she was conscious of another change which also made her tremulous; it was a sudden strange yearning of heart towards Will Ladislaw.*

In these lines we feel the vertigo of a mind grappling with a radical revision of recent history, a revision that in turn suggests new possibilities for the future. This transformation—"a metamorphosis in which memory would not adjust itself to the stirring of new organs"—sets the stage for the decision that will hover over the rest of the novel: whether to obey the dictates of the dead hand or sacrifice her estate—and confirm her late husband's worst suspicions—by marrying Will Ladislaw.

In the hands of a novelist like Jane Austen, those variables would have been sufficient to drive the narrative forward: Will she follow her heart and run off with Ladislaw, or make the financially smart decision and retain control of Lowick Manor? Framed in those terms, Dorothea's choice would have effectively been a dual-band decision, a choice between emotion and economics. Instead, Eliot turns Dorothea's choice into a full-spectrum affair, shaped by threadlike pressures from all the different scales of social experience.

Unlike Austen's heroines—many of whom have great independence of spirit and intelligence, but no professional ambition— Dorothea has a legitimate career in her sights: overseeing the development of Lowick Manor with a progressive agenda, building what we would now call low-income housing on the property. "I have delightful plans," she tells her sister. "I should like to take a great deal of land, and drain it, and make a little colony, where everybody should work, and all the work should be done well. I should know every one of the people and be their friend." Dorothea's ambitions for Lowick flow out of new intellectual currents that had widened the banks of political opinion in the second and third decades of the nineteenth century, specifically the cooperative movement pioneered by the Welsh socialist Robert Owen. When Austen's characters speak about "improvements" to their estates, at the turn of the century, the changes proposed are almost entirely in the service of making the property more economically efficient by adopting modern agricultural techniques. A generation later, Dorothea has her mind set on improving the lives of her tenants.

Dorothea hires a local estate manager named Caleb Garth to assist her in executing her plan for Lowick. Perhaps the saintliest figure in the book, Garth is rebounding from a failed attempt to become what we would now call a real estate developer, building and leasing out his own properties. When we first meet him, he is scraping by as a land surveyor, snubbed by some of the wealthier families in town who had once been his peers. The prospect of managing the Lowick estate offers a significant opportunity for Garth to get back on sound financial footing. But Dorothea's need for Garth has other historical roots beyond the ideologies of cooperative movement. The two are also bound together by the most dramatic technological development of the decade:

> With this good understanding between them, it was natural that Dorothea asked Mr. Garth to undertake any business connected with the three farms and the numerous tenements attached to Lowick Manor; indeed, his expectation of getting work for two was being fast fulfilled. As he said, "Business breeds." And one form of business which was beginning to breed just then was the construction of railways. A projected line was to run through Lowick parish where the cattle had hitherto grazed in a peace unbroken by astonishment; and thus it happened that the infant struggles of the railway system entered into the affairs of Caleb Garth, and determined the course of this history with regard to two persons who were dear to him.

The reform era enters into Dorothea's decision through her attraction to Will Ladislaw as well, who ends up editing a local paper purchased by Dorothea's uncle, Mr. Brooke, as a vehicle for

Brooke's somewhat muddled reformist ideals. As Dorothea begins to recognize her own talents and passion for progressive politics, Ladislaw becomes an intellectual ally as well as a paramour, and thus adds a further layer to her potential betrayal were she to marry him, given Casaubon's conservative politics. This slice of the spectrum illustrates yet another reason why hard choices are so challenging: even if Dorothea were to prioritize her political values over all the other conflicting scales, the decision would be perplexing. If she runs off with Ladislaw, she can support *his* political ambitions, but would lose direct control of her own ambitions to reform and improve Lowick. Which path will in the end lead to more of the social change she wishes to see in the world? The balance sheet between the two scenarios is not easily calculated.

Always in *Middlemarch*, beneath all the high-minded reforms, economic struggles, and moments of passion and camaraderie, an unrelenting murmur of town gossip can be heard in the background, subtly framing the decisions that confront the main characters, as we saw in Lydgate's anxiety about appearing to have sold out to Bulstrode in the vote for the new vicar. Despite their platonic history, for Dorothea to marry Ladislaw would be effectively to admit to the Middlemarch community that Casaubon's suspicions had been correct all along.

At its core, Dorothea's choice is a simple binary: Should she marry Ladislaw or not? But Eliot allows us to see the rich web of influence and consequence that surrounds that decision. A full-spectrum map of the novel would look something like this:

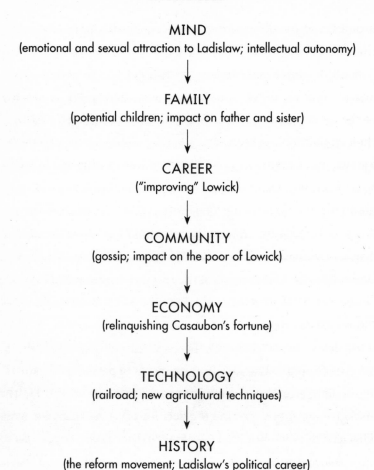

MIND
(emotional and sexual attraction to Ladislaw; intellectual autonomy)

↓

FAMILY
(potential children; impact on father and sister)

↓

CAREER
("improving" Lowick)

↓

COMMUNITY
(gossip; impact on the poor of Lowick)

↓

ECONOMY
(relinquishing Casaubon's fortune)

↓

TECHNOLOGY
(railroad; new agricultural techniques)

↓

HISTORY
(the reform movement; Ladislaw's political career)

In *Middlemarch*, each of these different levels plays a defining role in the story. There are great love affairs woven throughout the novel (Fred Vincy and Mary Garth, Dorothea and Will Ladislaw), but those romantic affiliations are only part of the story. Those emotional connections share the stage with the scientific revolutions that propel Lydgate's research, the coming of the railroad, and the epic political reforms of 1832. Compare *Middlemarch* to earlier classics from writers like Jane Austen or the

Brontës, and the difference is almost immediately apparent. The emotional and familial sphere in, say, *Pride and Prejudice* or *Jane Eyre* is fully developed; we are granted access to the rich psychological inner life of the central characters, though without some of the extravagance of Eliot's prose. (We see characters making choices, but don't get ten pages on their internal rumination the way we do at points in *Middlemarch*.) But the forces at play in those decisions are limited to the upper realm of the scale diagram: the emotional connection between two lovers, and the approval or disapproval of their immediate family and a handful of neighbors. From a modern critical perspective, we can detect larger, historical forces that frame the events of the narrative (the "improvements" of industrialized agriculture in Austen's time, the off-screen trauma of British colonialism in *Jane Eyre*), but those agents do not play a conscious role in either the deliberations of the characters or the editorial observations of the author herself. As brilliant and entertaining as Jane Austen's narratives are, their natural home is the drawing room, or the cotillion. That is the scale at which those stories operate. *Middlemarch* never lets its reader (or its characters) settle too comfortably into those drawing-room conversations. There is always a larger, bustling world banging on the windows.

MARY ANN'S CHOICE

The weight of public shame and scandal that plays into Dorothea's decision had direct biographical roots in Eliot's own experience, in a decision she had wrestled with personally more than two decades before she began writing *Middlemarch*. In October

1851, Eliot—known then by her real name, Mary Ann Evans—met the writer G. H. Lewes in a bookstore off Piccadilly Circus, a meeting that would set in motion one of the great—if unorthodox—emotional and creative collaborations of the nineteenth century. The relationship faced some formidable hurdles at the outset. Lewes was himself already in a complicated open marriage, and his initial chemistry with Eliot was unpromising. Shortly after the meeting, Eliot mocked Lewes's appearance in a letter. (According to one of Eliot's biographers, Lewes was "famously ugly, with wispy light-brown hair, a straggly moustache, pitted skin, a red, wet mouth and a head that looked too large for his small body.") But over time, a profound bond developed between the two intellectuals. Two years after their first meeting, Eliot wrote to a friend that Lewes "has quite won my liking, in spite of myself." Lewes would later look back on their courtship and remark in a journal entry from 1859, "To know her was to love her, and since then my life has been a new birth." By the summer of 1853, Lewes was visiting Eliot during her six-week holiday at St. Leonard's on the southern coast of England. Sometime during that sojourn, the two appear to have begun contemplating a momentous decision, one that would ultimately scandalize London society—and lay the groundwork for what many consider to be the finest novel ever written in the English language. They began to discuss living together as man and wife, without ever, officially, becoming man and wife.

It was, on the face of it, an impossible choice, thanks to the peculiarities of Victorian mores, in which the lines between what was permissible and what was forbidden were gerrymandered into contortions that largely allowed men exceptional sexual and romantic freedom and severely limited the options of women. Divorce was not legal except in the most extreme of circumstances. If Eliot wanted to become Lewes's life partner, she would have to surrender all the other aspects of her rich and promising life: the web of relationships she had established among the London intelligentsia, her promising career as a writer and translator. She had spent nearly a decade cementing a reputation as the most brilliant woman in England; now, to make a home with the man she loved, she would have to surrender all of that and become that most misogynistic of Victorian tropes: the fallen woman.

As Eliot contemplated her choice by the seaside in the summer of 1853, it must have seemed as though she faced a crossroads where both paths led, inevitably, to bleak destinations. Either she gave up the love of her life, or she gave up everything else she loved in her life. She could abandon the idea of living with Lewes, or she could renounce her position as a London intellectual, sever ties with her family and friends, and disappear into the hidden shame of the fallen woman.

But in the end, Eliot's choice, like most decisions of this magnitude, turned out to be a false binary. It was not a forking path after all. It took almost a year to discern it, but eventually Eliot and Lewes managed to find another route out of their impasse. After a six-month trip to the continent, where they gave cohabitation a trial run under the less moralizing eyes of the German and French intellectual elite, they returned to London and concocted an entirely novel solution to the problem of how to live together. Lewes negotiated an arrangement with his wife where she sanctioned Lewes sharing a home with Evans. Evans herself adopted Lewes's last name, and instructed her friends to address her using the Lewes surname in all their correspondence. (The shared surname helped them get past the suspicious eyes of their landladies.) Evans, over time, developed a rich and genuinely maternal relationship with Lewes's children. And as her literary ambition shifted toward the novel, she began publishing under the nom de plume "George Eliot," which kept her public work far from the scandal of her illicit alliance with Lewes.

In the end, they lived together virtually as man and wife for almost twenty-five years, ending with Lewes's death in 1878. Their actions were met with controversy and disapprobation, to be sure. The partnership with Lewes introduced strains into Eliot's relationship with her extended family that never fully healed. "I am sure you retain enough friendship and sisterly affection for me to be glad that I should have a kind husband to love me and take care of me," she wrote to her sister, who responded by cutting off all communication with Eliot. Many of their allies in London's progressive circles feared that their open immorality would do damage to their shared political causes. But over time, an unlikely aura of domestic normalcy settled over the couple. Sustained by the relationship, Eliot embarked on one of the great stretches of artistic productivity in modern history. "My life has deepened unspeakably during the last year," she wrote in 1857, just as that creative stretch was beginning. "I feel a greater capacity for moral and intellectual enjoyment, a more acute sense of my deficiencies in the past, a more solemn desire to be faithful to coming duties, than any I remember at any former period of my life."

THE FULL-SPECTRUM NOVEL

Both Mary Ann Evans and her fictional creation Dorothea Brooke confronted decisions that ranged across multiple scales. Mary Ann's choice originated with emotional and sexual feelings for Lewes, of course, but the ultimate ramifications of the choice involved many other parts of the spectrum: Evans's professional ambition as a writer and thinker; the politics of her embryonic feminism, carving out a career as an intellectual in a world dominated almost exclusively by men; the potential shame of becoming the subject of tittering gossip in drawing rooms and coffee houses throughout London; the familial ties that would no doubt be sundered by such a scandalous choice. Even mundane economics played into the decision. Evans and Lewes supported themselves with their writing. If they chose to spend the rest of their lives in sin, their livelihoods were in peril, too—Evans's most of all.

Dorothea's decision, seen from a full-spectrum perspective, has meaningful signal on at least five distinct bands. It is an emotional choice, of course: whether to marry the man she loves. But it is also a moral choice, bound up in her obligations to her late husband, however distrustful his codicil had revealed him to be. Like almost every marriage plot in the nineteenth-century novel, it is a financial choice, tied to an inheritance, with significant implications for Dorothea's economic standing. The fact that the economics are tied to the estate Dorothea dreams of improving means it is also a deeply political choice, shaped by the new intellectual ideas just emerging at that moment in history. And it is a choice framed by the stark possibility of shame and exile from the community she belongs to, in this case a small provincial town, with all its "frustrating complexity."

To make matters even more complicated, the decision is bound to set in motion a chain of future events that will shape the lives of many people beyond Dorothea and Ladislaw. You can measure the different bands in terms of the relative numbers of individual people they influence. The emotional level belongs to two lovers and their immediate family, gossip implicates hundreds, while political movements and reform ideologies shape and are shaped by thousands of lives. Giving up Lowick could threaten Caleb Garth's growing trade as an estate manager, thus threatening the budding romance between Fred and Mary; it would certainly affect the living conditions of Lowick's farmers and working poor. But perhaps Dorothea can do more good in the world by supporting Ladislaw's career as a man in a world where, for better but most likely for worse, men control the political conversation. The choice cannot be reduced down to a simple list of pros and cons because the downstream effects of the decision are so difficult to predict. Would her emotional (and presumably sexual, though of course Eliot is typically restrained on that dimension) happiness as Ladislaw's wife ultimately satisfy her enough to make up for the loss of her community and her social aspirations for Lowick? Will Ladislaw's efforts in the political arena ultimately counterbalance the damage she might do to the tenants at Lowick by abandoning her plans?

Ironically, for many readers of *Middlemarch*, the choice that Dorothea ultimately makes turns out to be the least inventive element of the entire book. She runs off with Ladislaw, abandons her social projects at Lowick, and supports his political career as a wife and mother of two children. Eliot defends her less ambitious path in the novel's famous closing lines: "But the effect of her being on those around her was incalculably diffusive: for the growing good of the world is partly dependent on unhistoric acts; and that things are not so ill with you and me as they might have been, is half owing to the number who lived faithfully a hidden life, and rest in unvisited tombs." In a novel filled with so much formal inventiveness, with a character so clearly pushing at the boundaries of conventional female heroes, Dorothea's choice strikes many critics as being more conventional than one would have expected, certainly more conventional than the choice that Mary Ann Evans herself made, in concocting an entirely sui generis definition of marriage with Lewes. The novelist was, in real life, more imaginative than her imaginary creation.

But the fact that Eliot found such rich complication in the "hidden life" of a figure like Dorothea is also what makes the novel so important. Just because your life may not be as heroic or world-changing as Darwin's or Eliot's doesn't mean the decisions you face in that life are not full spectrum. This is partly what the realist novel brought to the forefront of human consciousness: that ordinary lives were fascinating, too, if you looked at them with enough perspicacity. Admittedly, Dorothea's life, even with her more conventional last act, could hardly be called ordinary. But think of Lydgate and the threadlike pressures influencing the decision to replace the vicar. That could be any of us, wresting with a fraught decision to switch schools for one of your kids, or debating whether to take a job offer in a new city.

Recall that extraordinary passage from *Middlemarch* where Dorothea discovers the shocking reality of Casaubon's will: "Her world was in a state of convulsive change," Eliot writes; "the only thing she could say distinctly to herself was, that she must wait and think anew." Whatever approach we decide to take when making decisions of this magnitude, those two imperatives stand out: wait, and think anew. We can do the math of linear value modeling, or build scenarios in our heads, or sketch out a chart of impact pathways, or hold our own private charrettes. But whatever approach seems to work best—given the unique situation we are confronting, and our own distinctive mental habits and aptitudes—the two things we will almost always benefit from are time and a fresh perspective.

OTHER MINDS

Novels like *Middlemarch* do not give us simple prescriptions for making the complex decisions of our own lives. They are not simple morality plays. The trick of making complex decisions does not lie in a set of invariable rules, because every complex decision, by definition, is unique. All the techniques we have explored in the preceding chapters ultimately involve strategies for *perceiving* the decision map more clearly, understanding its singular characteristics, and not getting stuck in familiar habits of thought or preconceived models. Great novels—or at least novels that are not didactic in their moralizing—give us something fundamentally similar to what we get out of the simulations of war games or ensemble forecasts: they let us experience parallel lives, and see the complexity of those experiences in vivid detail. They let us see the choice in all its intricacy. They map all the thread-like pressures; they chart the impact pathways as the choice ripples through families, communities, and the wider society. They give us practice, not prepackaged instructions.

It is not an accident that so many of these tools and strategies that help us wrestle with complex decisions revolve around story-telling. Running multiple simulations of experience, imagining alternate realities—these are ancient practices, as old as myth and folklore. The evolutionary psychologists John Tooby and Leda Cosmides have convincingly argued that our appetite for fictional narrative is not just the result of cultural invention, but instead has deep roots in the evolutionary history of the human brain. Echoing the complaints of the teenage Mary Ann Evans about the frivolous escapism of novels ("Have I then any time to spend on things that never existed?"), Tooby and Cosmides begin with a puzzle: Why do people willingly spend so much time (and money) exploring events and experiences that are, by definition, *not true?*

> [O]*rganisms should have an appetite for obtaining accurate information, and the distinction between true information and false information should be important in determining whether the information is absorbed or disregarded. This "appetite for the true" model spectacularly fails to predict large components of the human appetite for information. When given a choice, most individuals prefer to read novels over textbooks, and prefer films depicting fictional events over documentaries. That is, they remain intensely interested in communications that are explicitly marked as false. The familiarity of this phenomenon hides its fundamental strangeness.*

Why do people waste so many cognitive cycles contemplating information that is demonstrably false? Part of the answer is that human intelligence actually depends on varying hypothetical degrees of truth and falsity. The simple black-and-white distinction between the two realms is actually much blurrier. Even without getting into postmodern theories of truth and its social construction, in everyday life, human brains shuffle across a vast gradient of truth. Tooby and Cosmides describe some of them: "the might-be-true, the true-over-there, the once-was-true, the what-others-believe-is-true, the true-only-if-I-did-that, the not-true-here, the what-they-want-me-to-believe-is-true, the will-someday-be-true, the certainly-is-not-true, the what-he-told-me, the seems-true-on-the-basis-of-these claims, and on and on." Being able to bounce back and forth between those different regions of truth is not a sign of nihilism. It is, instead, the sign of a discerning, imaginative mind.

Stories exercise and rehearse that faculty for juggling different frames of truth, in part because they themselves occupy a complicated position on the map of truth and falsehood, and in part because stories often involve us observing other (fictional) beings going through their own juggling act. When Casaubon adds the damning codicil to his will, he is working in the realm of the might-someday-be-true. When Dorothea worries about the town gossips' reaction to her marrying Ladislaw, she is exploring the what-others-believe-is-true framework.

Stories serve a function not unlike the ensemble forecasts of modern meteorology. When Lewis Fry Richardson first proposed his "Weather Prediction by Numerical Process," the approach was limited by the bottleneck of pre-digital calculation; the weather itself changed faster than anyone could complete the "numerical process" for predicting it. Weather forecasting dramatically improved its accuracy once computers were fast enough to generate hundreds or thousands of iterations of the same forecast, playing out all the various scenarios and looking for patterns in the results. Fictional narratives offer a similar boost. By telling one another stories, we free ourselves from the bottleneck of an individual life. Stories, as Tooby and Cosmides put it, mean we "are no longer limited by the slow and unreliable flow of actual experience. Instead, we can immerse ourselves in the comparatively rapid flow of vicarious, orchestrated, imagined, or fictional experience. A hunter-gatherer band might contain scores or even hundreds of lifetimes' worth of experience whose summary can be tapped into if it can be communicated . . . With fiction unleashing our reactions to potential lives and realities, we feel more richly and adaptively about what we have not actually experienced. This allows us not only to understand others' choices and inner lives better, but to feel our way . . . to better choices ourselves." In a sense, you can see the appetite for fictional narratives as an extension of the "openness to experience" trait that was so prominent in Philip Tetlock's successful forecasters. Novels and biographical histories allow us to open a kind of perceptual door into other people's experiences, to live vicariously through the unique challenges of their existence, watch them from the inside as they wrestle with their own hard choices.

That capacity to project into the "inner lives" of other people is of course a central requirement in most important personal decisions. When Lewes and Evans contemplated their future life outside the boundaries of acceptable Victorian morality, a significant part of the decision revolved around the imagined reactions of other people: the close ties of friends and family and colleagues; the weaker ties of the social milieu they traveled in. Evaluating the potential consequences of their actions demanded that they project themselves into the thoughts and emotions and moral codes of these people. Would Evans's family reject her, or would they eventually make peace with her "alternative" lifestyle with Lewes? Would the chattering classes of London be so scandalized by the relationship that the couple would be forced to move elsewhere, or would the gossip quickly move on to another story and leave Evans and Lewes in relative peace?

Psychologists and cognitive scientists refer to this ability to imagine the subjective life of other people as having a "theory of mind." People vary a great deal in their other-mindedness. People on the autistic and Asperger's side of the autism spectrum are usually challenged in their ability to conjure up these mental models; their brains seem less likely to instinctively speculate on what other people are thinking. But most of us can run these mental simulations so quickly that we don't even notice we're doing it. We notice the subtle raised eyebrow of the supervisor we're talking to and we automatically build a mental simulation of what she might be thinking: *Is she skeptical about the point I'm trying to make? Am I confusing her?*

For hard choices, of course, that rapid-fire mental modeling has to leave the realm of instinct and become a more deliberate affair. Just as we have to mentally simulate what we think will happen to the real estate market in the neighborhood we're contemplating moving to, we also have to simulate the emotional responses that the move will trigger in the people close to us. Will the kids make friends quickly at their new school, or will they struggle in the first months without a preexisting network around them? Will your partner be frustrated by the longer commute to work? As with so many elements of the hard choice, there are few generalizable rules that govern those simulated minds. We are all fingerprints. But what *is* generalizable is the importance of building those mental models, taking the time to think through the subjective responses of the individuals influenced by the decision at hand.

In the months that passed as I assembled my case for the California move, I was effectively writing a story myself, a story about how this westward migration would delight and strengthen our family—give the kids a richer connection to nature, force us all to build a different mental map of what "home" meant. But in all honesty, I never bothered to construct an *alternate* story. Right before we bought the house we eventually moved into, a quirky little storybook-style cottage with a small garden up on a hill overlooking the bay, I took my father to see it. I was certain he would find it as intoxicating as I did. But he seemed more worried than exuberant, and afterward, he called me and tried to talk me out of buying it. "Lexie's going to get really lonely up on that hill," he said prophetically, about my wife's future response to California living. But I dismissed it as a father's usual concern over any big change in his child's life.

We were both building scenario plans, but my father was doing something else as well: he was running a premortem. And it was a premortem based on a sensitivity to how the decision might play out from my wife's point of view. That empathy, that knack for peering into another person's mind and imagining how some theoretical event might feel, is almost by definition one of the most important virtues in making complex decisions. If the point is to calculate the greatest happiness for the greatest number, what better skill than the ability to predict the presence or absence of happiness in other people's minds? Some might argue that empathy as a trait is less vital when decisions take on a mass scale, since it is not always useful to condense down a thousand or a million mental states into a much smaller group of "average" mind-sets. Most empathy is grounded in the granular connection to people we know, face-to-face. But for personal decisions, like our California move, empathy lets you run the projection cycles much faster if you genuinely know the person into whose mind you are projecting.

This is the other reason reading novels turns out to enhance our decision-making skills. A few years ago, a pair of scientists at the New School in Manhattan published a study in *Science* that quickly became a viral sensation on social media, particularly among former humanities majors. The study assigned a range of reading materials—popular fiction, literary fiction, and nonfiction—to a group of subjects, and then evaluated whether the reading improved their "theory of mind" skills. The study found no change in the subjects who had read popular fiction or nonfiction, but detected a statistically meaningful improvement in other-mindedness after reading even a small amount of literary fiction. Subsequent experiments have failed to replicate the effect, but many studies have confirmed that a lifelong habit of reading literary fiction correlates strongly with enhanced theory of mind skills. We don't know if other-minded people are drawn to literary fiction, or if the act of reading actually improves their abilities to build those mental models. Most likely, it is a bit of both. But whatever the causal relationship, it is clear that one of the defining experiences of reading literary novels involves the immersion in an alternate subjectivity. Cinema and photography can take you to other worlds with more visual fidelity; music can excite our bodies and our emotions. But no form rivals the novel's ability to project us into the interior landscape of other minds.

Eliot saw that projection as a kind of moral imperative.

"There is no general doctrine which is not capable of eating out our morality if unchecked by the deep-seated habit of direct fellow-feeling with individual fellow-men," she observes at one point in *Middlemarch*. As Rebecca Mead writes, "Her credo might be expressed this way: If I really care for you—if I try to think myself into your position and orientation—then my world is bettered by my effort at understanding and comprehension." The novel is an empathy machine. That act of mental projection presumably strengthens the ties between us, in the moral view that Eliot took of it. But that ability also makes us better decision-makers. We can imagine all sorts of half-truths and hypotheticals: what-she-will-think-if-this-happens, what-he-thinks-I'm-feeling. Reading literary novels trains the mind for that kind of analysis. You can't run a thousand parallel simulations of your own life, the way the meteorologists do, but you can read a thousand novels over the course of that life. It's true that the stories that unfold in those novels do not directly mirror the stories of our own lives. Most of us will never confront a choice between our late husband's estate and matrimonial bliss with our radical lover. But the point of reading this kind of literary fiction is not to acquire a ready-made formula for your own hard choices. If you are contemplating that move to the suburbs, *Middlemarch* doesn't tell you what to do. No form of outside advice—whether it takes the form of a novel or a cognitive science study or a pop-psychology paperback—can tell you what to do in these kinds of situations, because these situations contain, by definition, their own unique configuration of threadlike pressures. What the novel—along with some of the other forms of mapping and simulating that we have explored—*does* teach you to do is to see the situation with what Eliot called "a keen vision and feeling," and keep you from the tendency to "walk about well wadded with stupidity." The novel doesn't give you answers. But it does make you better at following the threads.

THE NOVEL AND THE DEFAULT NETWORK

If you are interested in exploring the full-spectrum complexity of a decision—from the inner life of the participants all the way out to the realm of gossip or technological change—no artistic form has ever rivaled the depth and breadth of novels like *Middlemarch*. (Nonfiction biography and history are their only peers.) Capturing the hard choice on all the scales of experience that are implicated in it; following the threadlike pressures from mind to mind, from drawing room to town square; taking us from the inner life of the decision-maker to the vast sweep of generational change—these are not just a few reasons we happen to read novels, among many others. They are what the novel does best.

In a way, you can think of the novel itself as a kind of technology. Like most technologies, it builds on and enhances existing skills that human beings possess. Novels—along with other long-form arts like movies or serial-narrative television—are an amplified version of the default network's instinctual storytelling. The novel is to the daydreams of the default network what the Hubble telescope is to our visual system. They are all tools that let us see farther and deeper. Over millions of years of evolution, our brains developed a predilection for running through imagined futures, anticipating the emotional reactions of people close to us, sketching out the potential consequences—all in the service of making better decisions in the present. That knack for speculative untruths—made-up stories about how it all might turn out if you choose this path over that one—gave us the wisdom of *Homo prospectus*. And over time, we developed cultural forms that allowed us to make ever more elaborate simulations: first as myths and legends, passed down through oral tradition, and then as the full-spectrum narrative of the novel, following the paths of imaginary people as they wrestled with the decisions that would define their lives. More than any other creative form, novels give us an opportunity to simulate and rehearse the hard choices of life before we actually make one ourselves. They give us an unrivaled vista into the interior life of someone wrestling with a complex, multilayered choice, even if the choice itself happens to be a fictional one. The ensemble runs of the weather forecasters are fiction, too: in some runs, the hurricane veers left and spares the mainland; in others, it bears down on the coastal cities with devastating force. We can better predict which path the real hurricane will take—and thus which path we should take ourselves to avoid it—because the computers that generate those ensemble forecasts are such able fabulists, stringing together thousands of alternative narratives in a matter of minutes. The novel gives us a different kind of simulation. Not the long view of climate change, or even the short-term view of a tropical storm, but something more intimate: the path of a human life, changing and being changed by the world that surrounds it.

WE MIGHT AS WELL GET GOOD AT IT

I spent most of the first quarter century of my life in school, and I don't remember one class over that entire stretch where decision-making itself was on the syllabus. My teachers taught me grammar, chemistry, algebra, European history, postmodern literary theory, film studies—but not *once* did a teacher stand at the lectern and explain how to make a farsighted choice. I'm not the sort of person who gripes about all the useless trivia I learned in school; I've made a career out of finding meaning in the obscure realms of different disciplines. But I wish at least some of that time in the classroom had been dedicated to the art of deciding.

It is true that the brain science and philosophical implications behind the way we decide will regularly appear on the syllabi of Cognitive Science or Psych 101, or in electives on, say, the utilitarians. And business schools regularly feature entire courses on the topic, most of them focused on administrative or executive decisions. But you will almost never find a required course dedicated to the subject in even the most progressive high school. Are there more important skills than the ability to make hard choices? I can think of a few rivals: creativity, empathy, resilience. But surely complex decision-making has to rank near the top of the list. It is at the very heart of what we mean when we use words like "wisdom." So why isn't it an anchor tenant in our schools?

The nice thing about a field like decision science or decision theory—or whatever name you want to give to it—is that the field is a sort of intellectual chameleon: it plays well in a highbrow context, and in a pragmatic one. There's a deep well of philosophical literature and a growing body of neuroscience research that wrestle with the problem, but it's also a problem with immediate practical utility for everyone. Who doesn't want to make better choices?

There's a pedagogical argument for this approach as well. Framing an entire course around the farsighted decision actually has the potential to light up interest in other fields that can sometimes seem dry when they are quarantined off in their traditional disciplinary silos. The default network, for instance, might come up as a sidebar in a sophomore biology survey, during the unit on neurology. In that context, it's just another set of facts to memorize: *today, it's the default network; tomorrow, we're covering neurotransmitters; next week, we move on to the amygdala.* But put the default network in a class that's explicitly designed to teach you how to make better decisions, and suddenly the whole idea of daydreaming as a cognitively rich activity takes on new relevance. You don't have to be planning a career as a brain surgeon to find it *useful* to learn about this strange superpower that was only revealed by overactive PET scans.

What fields would such a syllabus incorporate? Certainly it would involve the study of history, moral philosophy, behavioral

economics, probability, neurology, computer science, and literature. The course itself would be a case study in the power of diverse perspectives. But beyond the multidisciplinary sweep,
students would learn a series of techniques that they could then
apply to their own lives and careers: how to build a full-spectrum
map of a complex decision; how to design a scenario plan and a
premortem; how to build a values model and Bad Events Table.
They'd learn the importance of sharing hidden profiles among
diverse groups, and the value of measuring uncertainty. They'd
learn to seek out undiscovered options and to avoid the tendency
to fall back into narrowband assessments. They'd learn the importance of being other-minded, and how reading great literature can help enhance that faculty. No doubt there are a thousand
electives out there—in high schools and college humanities programs, not to mention business schools—that dabble in some of
these themes. But why not bring them into the core?

The other case for bringing decision-making into the classroom is that it provides a valuable bridge between the sciences
and the humanities. When you read philosophy in the context of
the promise and peril of superintelligent machines, you can see
immediately how seemingly abstract ideas about logic and ethics
can have material effects on our technological future. When you
read literature as an exercise in improving our ability to make
farsighted decisions, you can appreciate the way novels mirror the
scientific insights that arise from randomized controlled studies
and ensemble forecasts, in their shared reliance on the power of
simulation to expand our perspectives, challenge our assumptions, and propose new possibilities. This is not a matter of "reducing" the humanities down to scientific data. For the most
intimate decisions, novels endow us with wisdom that science

cannot, by definition, provide. When my wife and I were con-templating our California move, we couldn't somehow run a controlled experiment and send dozens of comparable couples off to the West Coast, then wait around for a few years crunching the data on their future happiness. You don't get to run ensemble simulations on your own life. Storytelling is what we have as a substitute.

Of course, the reverse is also true: science gives us insights that novels cannot provide. When Joyce and Faulkner and Woolf invented stream of consciousness as a literary device, they helped us perceive the strange habits of mind wandering, but it was the PET and fMRI scans of the default network that allowed us to see, for the first time, just how powerful that kind of cognition really is. Behavioral psychology and mock juries and cognitive neuroscience have all helped us perceive the challenges posed by farsighted decisions more clearly, particularly on the scale of the small group. Novels just happen to shine a different kind of light. We see farther when both lights are on.

Acknowledgments

Appropriately enough—given the subject matter—this book was a long time in the making. I first started taking notes on the topic of complex decision-making almost ten years ago, and it took me a full five years to get from the initial proposal to a first draft of the manuscript. Consequently, I am even more grateful than usual to my publisher, editor, and agent—Geoffrey Kloske, Courtney Young, and Lydia Wills, respectively—for having faith in this project over that extended period, and for convincing me that this book was important to write when I had my doubts. A special thanks to Courtney for her stellar editorial guidance: challenging my arguments where they deserved challenging, suggesting new avenues to explore, deftly reminding me at points that this was a book about decision-making and not a literary monograph on the late works of George Eliot. As always, I am very lucky to be a part of the extended Riverhead family: thanks to Kevin Murphy, Katie Freeman, Lydia Hurt, Jessica White, and Kate Stark for all their help bringing this book into the world.

This book was also greatly improved thanks to many conversations with friends and experts over the past decade: Eric Liftin,

ACKNOWLEDGMENTS

Rufus Griscom, Mark Bailey, Denise Caruso, Doug Vakoch, Kathryn Denning, Betsey Schmidt, David Brin, Frank Drake, Paul Hawken, Scott Klemmer, Peter Leyden, Ken Goldberg. My old friends at the Long Now Foundation—especially Stewart Brand, Kevin Kelly, Alexander Rose, Peter Schwartz, and Brian Eno—were an inspiration from the very beginning of this project. Special thanks to Zander for introducing me to the METI project, and to my editors at the *New York Times Magazine*, Bill Wasik and Jake Silvertstein, for allowing me to explore the epic decision of METI at such length in the magazine. Thanks to Wes Neff and the team at the Leigh Bureau for introducing me to so many interesting people and industries over the years, some of which found their way into this book. My wife Alexa Robinson—my partner in so many long-term decisions—gave the book an astute edit in the late stages. Our sons—Clay, Rowan, and Dean—are a constant reminder of the importance of keeping your eye on the long view.

This book is dedicated to my father, master of the pre-mortem and wise counsel for every major decision I've faced in my life.

Brooklyn
March 2018

Bibliography

Anbinder, Tyler. *Five Points: The 19th-Century New York City Neighborhood That Invented Tap Dance, Stole Elections, and Became the World's Most Notorious Slum.* New York: Free Press, 2001.

Anderson, Katherine. *Predicting the Weather: Victorians and the Science of Meteorology.* Chicago: University of Chicago Press, 2010.

Armitage, Peter. "Fisher, Bradford Hill, and Randomization." *International Journal of Epidemiology*, 32 (2003): 925–928.

Baron, Jonathan. *Thinking and Deciding.* New York: Cambridge University Press, 2008.

Bentham, Jeremy. "An Introduction to the Principles of Morals and Legislation." www.econlib.org/library/Bentham/bnthPML1.html.

Bergen, Peter L. *Manhunt: the Ten-Year Search for Bin Laden from 9/11 to Abbottabad.* New York: Crown/Archetype, 2012.

Bowden, Mark. *The Finish: The Killing of Osama bin Laden.* New York: Grove/Atlantic, Inc., 2012.

Brand, Stewart. *The Clock of the Long Now: Time and Responsibility.* New York: Basic Books, 1999.

Browne, Janet. *Charles Darwin: Voyaging.* Princeton, NJ: Princeton University Press, 1996.

Buckner, Randy L. "The Serendipitous Discovery of the Brain's Default Network." *Neuroimage* (2011).

Burch, Druin. *Taking the Medicine: A Short History of Medicine's Beautiful Idea, and Our Difficulty Swallowing It.* London: Vintage, 2010

Chernow, Ron. *Washington: A Life.* New York: Penguin Press, 2010.

Christian, Brian, and Tom Griffiths. *Algorithms to Live By: The Computer Science of Human Decisions.* Grand Haven, MI: Brilliance Audio, 2016.

"Defense Science Board Task Force on the Role and Status of DoD Red Teaming Activities." *Office of the Under Secretary of Defense*, (2003).

Dobbs, Michael. *One Minute to Midnight: Kennedy, Khrushchev, and Castro on the Brink of Nuclear War*. New York: Alfred A. Knopf, 2008.

Duer, William. *New-York as It Was During the Latter Part of the Last Century*. New York: Stanford and Swords, 1849.

Edwards, Paul N. "History of Climate Modeling." *Wiley Interdisciplinary Reviews: Climate* 2 (2011): 128–39.

Eliot, George. *Middlemarch*. MobileReference, 2008.

Feynman, Richard P. *The Meaning of It All: Thoughts of a Citizen-Scientist*. New York: Basic Books, 2009.

Franklin, Benjamin. *Mr. Franklin: A Selection from His Personal Letters*. New Haven, CT: Yale University Press, 1956.

Gladwell, Malcolm. *Blink: The Power of Thinking Without Thinking*. Boston: Little, Brown and Company, 2007.

Gregory, Robin, Lee Failing, Michael Harstone, Graham Long, Tim McDaniels, and Dan Ohlson. *Structured Decision Making: A Practical Guide to Environmental Management Choices*. Hoboken, NJ: John Wiley & Sons, 2012.

Greicius, Micahel D., Ben Krasnow, Allan L. Reiss, and Vinod Menon. "Functional Connectivity in the Resting Brain: A Network Analysis of the Default Mode Hypothesis." *Proceedings of the National Academy of Sciences* 100 (2003): 253–58.

Gribbin, John, and Mary Gribbin. *FitzRoy: The Remarkable Story of Darwin's Captain and the Invention of the Weather Forecast*. ReAnimus Press, 2016.

Hawken, Paul, James A. Ogilvy, and Peter Schwartz. *Seven Tomorrows: Toward a Voluntary History*. New York: Bantam Books, 1982.

Heath, Chip, and Dan Heath. *Decisive: How to Make Better Choices in Life and Work*. New York: Crown Business, 2013.

Hughes, Kathryn. *George Eliot: The Last Victorian*. New York: HarperCollins Publishers, 2012.

Janis, Irving. *Victims of Groupthink: A Psychological Study of Foreign-Policy Decisions and Fiascoes*. Boston: Houghton, Mifflin, 1972.

Janis, Irving, and Leon Mann. *Decision Making: A Psychological Analysis of Conflict, Choice, and Commitment*. New York: The Free Press, 1977.

Johnston, Henry Phelps. *The Campaign of 1776 Around New York and Brooklyn: Including a New and Circumstantial Account of the Battle of Long Island and the Loss of New York, With a Review of Events to the Close of the Year: Containing Maps, Portraits, and Original Documents.* Cranbury, NJ: Scholars Bookshelf, 2005.

Kahneman, Daniel. *Thinking, Fast and Slow.* New York: Farrar, Straus and Giroux, 2011.

Keats, Jonathan. "Let's Play War: Could War Games Replace the Real Thing?" *Nautilus* 28 (September 24, 2015).

Keeney, Ralph L. "Value-Focused Thinking: Identifying Decision Opportunities and Creating Alternatives." *European Journal of Operational Research*, 92 (1996): 537–49.

Keith, Phil. *Stay the Rising Sun: The True Story of USS* Lexington, *Her Valiant Crew, and Changing the Course of World War II.* Minneapolis: Zenith Press, 2015.

Keynes, Randal. *Darwin, His Daughter, and Human Evolution.* New York: Penguin Publishing Group, 2002.

Kidd, David Comer, and Emanuele Castano. "Reading Literary Fiction Improves Theory of Mind." *Science* 342 (2013): 377–80.

Klein, Gary. *Sources of Power: How People Make Decisions.* Cambridge, MA: MIT Press, 1999.

Mead, Rebecca. *My Life in Middlemarch.* New York: Crown/Archetype, 2014.

Mitchell, Deborah J., J. Edward Russo, and Nancy Pennington. "Back to the Future: Temporal Perspective in the Explanation of Events." *Journal of Behavioral Decision Making* 2 (1989): 25–38.

Moore, Peter. "The Birth of the Weather Forecast." 66c.com, April 30, 2015. www.bbc.com/news/magazine-32483678.

Morson, Gary Saul, and Martin Schapiro. *Cents and Sensibility: What Economics Can Learn from the Humanities.* Princeton University Press. Kindle Edition.

Nutt, Paul C. *Making Tough Decisions: Tactics for Improving Managerial Decision Making.* San Francisco: Jossey-Bass Publishers, 1989.

———. *Why Decisions Fail: Avoiding the Blunders and Traps That Lead to Debacles.* San Francisco: Berrett-Koehler Publishers, 2002.

Raichle, Marcus E., and Abraham Z. Snyder. "A Default Mode of Brain

Function: A Brief History of an Evolving Idea." *Neuroimage* 37 (2007): 1083–90.

Raichle, Marcus E., Ann Mary MacLeod, Abraham Z. Snyder, William J. Powers, Debra A. Gusnard, and Gordon L. Shulman. "A Default Mode of Brain Function." *Proceedings of the National Academy of Sciences* 98 (2001): 676–82.

Regan, Helen M., Mark Colyvan, and Mark A. Burgman. "A Taxonomy and Treatment of Uncertainty for Ecology and Conservation Biology." *Ecological Applications* 12 (2002): 618–25.

Rejeski, David. "Governing on the Edge of Change." wilsoncenter.org, 2012.

Richardson, Lewis Fry. *Weather Prediction by Numerical Process.* Cambridge, Cambridge University Press, 1924.

Riddick, W. L. *Charrette Processes: A Tool In Urban Planning.* York, Pennsylvania: George Shumway, 1971.

Sanderson, Eric W. *Mannahatta: A Natural History of New York City.* New York: Abrams, 2009.

Schwartz, Peter. *The Art of the Long View.* New York: Random House, Inc., 2012.

Seligman, Martin E. P., Peter Railton, Roy F. Baumeister, and Chandra Sripada. *Homo Prospectus.* New York: Oxford University Press, 2016.

Simon, Herbert A. "Rational Decision Making in Business Organizations." In *Nobel Lectures, Economics 1969–1980.* Singapore: World Scientific Publishing, 1992.

Singer, Peter, and Katarzyna de Lazari-Radek. *Utilitarianism: A Very Short Introduction.* Oxford: Oxford University Press, Kindle edition.

Stasser, Garold, and Williams Titus. "Hidden Profiles: A Brief History." *Psychological Inquiry* 14 (2003): 304–313.

Stasser, Garold, Dennis D. Stewart, and Gwen M. Wittenbaum. "Expert Roles and Information Exchange During Discussion: The Importance of Knowing Who Knows What." *Journal of Experimental Social Psychology*, 31.

Steedman, Carolyn. "Going to Middlemarch: History and the Novel." *Michigan Quarterly Review* XL, 3 (2001).

Sunstein, Cass R., and Reid Hastie. *Wiser: Getting Beyond Groupthink to Make Groups Smarter.* Cambridge, MA: Harvard Business Review Press, 2014.

Swinton, William E. "The Hydrotherapy and Infamy of Dr. James Gully." *Canadian Medical Association Journal* 123 (1980): 1262–64.

Tetlock, Philip E., and Dan Gardner. *Superforecasting: The Art and Science of Prediction*. New York: Crown/Archetype, 2015.

Tooby, John, and Leda Cosmides. "Does Beauty Build Adapted Minds? Toward an Evolutionary Theory of Aesthetics, Fiction, and the Arts." *SubStance*, 94/95 (2001): 6–14.

Uglow, Jenny. *The Lunar Men: Five Friends Whose Curiosity Changed the World*. New York: Farrar, Straus and Giroux, 2002.

Vakoch, Douglas A., and Matthew F. Dowd. *The Drake Equation: Estimating the Prevalence of Extraterrestrial Life Through the Ages*. New York: Cambridge University Press, 2015.

Vohs, Kathleen D., Roy F. Baumeister, Brandon J. Schmeichel, Jean M. Twenge, Noelle M. Nelson, and Dianne M. Tice. "Making Choices Impairs Subsequent Self-Control: A Limited-Resource Account of Decision Making, Self-Regulation, and Active Initiative." *Journal of Personality and Social Psychology*, 94 (2008): 883–898.

Wack, Pierre. "Living in the Futures." *Harvard Business Review*, May 2013.

———. "Scenarios: Uncharted Waters Ahead." *Harvard Business Review* (September 1985).

Westfahl, Gary, Wong Kin Yuen, and Amy Kit-sze Chan, eds. *Science Fiction and the Prediction of the Future: Essays on Foresight and Fallacy*. Jefferson, NC: McFarland, 2011.

Wohlstetter, Roberta. *Pearl Harbor: Warning and Decision*. Stanford: Stanford University Press, 1962.

Yamin, Rebecca. "From Tanning to Tea: The Evolution of a Neighborhood." *Historical Archaeology* 35 (2001): 6–15.

Yoshioka, Alan. "Use of Randomisation in the Medical Research Council's Clinical Trial of Streptomycin in Pulmonary Tuberculosis in the 1940s." *BMJ*, 317 (1998): 1220–1223.

Zenko, Micah. *Red Team: How to Succeed by Thinking Like the Enemy*. New York: Basic Books, 2015.

Notes

INTRODUCTION: MORAL ALGEBRA

2 **"It was the grand resort"**: William Duer, *New-York as It Was During the Latter Part of the Last Century* (New York: Stanford and Swords, 1849), 13–14.

8 **Under the heading "Not Marry"**: Randal Keynes, *Darwin, His Daughter, and Human Evolution* (New York: Penguin Publishing Group, 2002), loc. 195–203, Kindle.

10 **"the Affair of so much Importance"**: *Mr. Franklin: A Selection from His Personal Letters* (New Haven, CT: Yale University Press, 1956).

14 **"Problem 1"**: Daniel Kahneman, *Thinking, Fast and Slow* (New York: Farrar, Straus and Giroux, 2011), loc. 4668–4672, Kindle.

23 **"One idea was to throw"**: Peter L. Bergen, *Manhunt: the Ten-Year Search for Bin Laden from 9/11 to Abbottabad* (New York: Crown/Archetype, 2012), loc. 1877, Kindle.

29 **deliberative decisions involve three steps:** Some decisions—jury decisions about guilt or innocence, the CIA's decision about who was living in that mysterious compound—do not involve the second predictive phase, given that they are not really about the consequences of taking one path versus another, but rather about a question of fact: Is he guilty or innocent? Is Osama bin Laden living in this house?

30 **"He did not like frustrating"**: George Eliot, *Middlemarch* (MobileReference, 2008), loc. 191., Kindle.

34 **the most meaningful moments of their lives:** The literary critic Gary Saul Morson describes this property of the novel—and of human experience itself—as "narrativeness," a way of measuring how readily a given phenomenon can be compressed down into a simple theory or maxim: "Although one could give a narrative explanation about the orbit of

Mars—first it was here, and then it moved there, and then it skidded in over here—it would be absurd to do so because Newton's laws already allow one to derive its location at any point in time. So I left the Center with a new concept in mind, which I called 'narrativeness.' Narrativeness, which comes in degrees, measures the need for narrative. In the example of Mars, there is zero narrativeness. On the other hand, the sort of ethical questions posed by the great realist novels have maximal narrativeness. When is there narrativeness? The more we need culture as a means of explanation, the more narrativeness. The more we invoke irreducibly individual human psychology, the more narrativeness. And the more contingent factors—events that are unpredictable from within one's disciplinary framework—play a role, the more narrativeness." (Morson, 38–39.)

1: MAPPING

42 **National Geospatial-Intelligence Agency:** "General James Cartwright, then the vice chairman of the Joint Chiefs, recalls, 'That was a good vehicle for us as we planned the various options to then sit down with that model and say . . . "This is how we would come at it; this is what would happen in this courtyard or this house. . . . Here's how we would have more than one avenue of approach on what we thought were the target-inhabited buildings."'" Bergen, 164–165.

49 **"aquatic habitat, terrestrial habitat":** Robin Gregory, Lee Failing, Michael Harstone, Graham Long, Tim McDaniels, and Dan Ohlson, *Structured Decision Making: A Practical Guide to Environmental Management Choices* (Hoboken, NJ: John Wiley & Sons, 2012), loc. 233–234, Kindle.

50 **Daniel Kahneman:** Kahneman, loc. 1388–1397.

51 **focus on *shared* information:** Cass R. Sunstein and Reid Hastie, *Wiser: Getting Beyond Groupthink to Make Groups Smarter* (Cambridge, MA: Harvard Business Review Press, 2014), loc. 280–287, Kindle.

51 **"Some group members are *cognitively central"*:** Sunstein and Hastie, loc. 1142–1149.

54 **non-whites in the jury room:** www.scientificamerican.com/article/how -diversity-makes-us-smarter, accessed Sept. 2016.

57 **"The whole pattern":** Gary Klein, *Sources of Power: How People Make Decisions* (Cambridge, MA: MIT Press, 1999), loc. 466–469, Kindle.

58 **"The fireman's internal computer":** Malcolm Gladwell, *Blink: The Power of Thinking Without Thinking* (Boston: Little, Brown and Company, 2007), loc. 1455–1461, Kindle.

60 **thirteen distinct species:** Helen M. Regan, Mark Colyvan, and Mark A Burgman, "A Taxonomy and Treatment of Uncertainty for Ecology and Conservation Biology," *Ecological Applications* 12, no. 2 (2002): 618–628. Gregory, et al, summarized the categories as follows: (knowledge) uncertainty "When we are uncertain about facts concerning events or outcomes in the world because . . . Natural variation . . . outcomes that vary naturally with respect to time, space or other variables and can be difficult to predict Measurement error . . . we cannot measure things precisely Systematic error . . . we have not calibrated our instruments or designed our experiments/sampling properly Model uncertainty . . . we do not know how things interact with each other Subjective judgment . . . we use judgment to interpret data, observations or experience. This results in uncertainty in individual judgments and uncertainty caused by differences across experts Sources of linguistic uncertainty When we are not communicating effectively because . . . Vagueness . . . language permits borderline cases. Vagueness can be numeric (how many 'tall' trees?, when does a population of algae become a 'bloom'?) or non-numeric (how to define habitat suitability?) Ambiguity . . . words have more than one meaning and it is not clear which is intended: 'natural' environment, forest 'cover' Context dependence . . . descriptions are not used in context; an oil spill that is 'big' on my driveway would be considered 'small' in the ocean Underspecificity . . . there is unwanted generality; 'it might rain tomorrow' vs 'there is a 70% probability of rain at location tomorrow' Indeterminacy . . . words used at one point in time mean something different." Gregory et al., loc. 123, Kindle.

62 *The Meaning of It All:* Richard P. Feynman, *The Meaning of It All: Thoughts of a Citizen-Scientist* (New York: Basic Books, 2009), loc. 26–27.

64 **"Brennan pushed them":** Bergen, loc. 134–135.

72 **And even when the idea:** In *Victims of Groupthink* (Boston: Houghton Mifflin, 1972), Irving Janis offers a case study analyzing the chain of oversight and false conviction that enabled the military commanders in Hawaii and Washington to be blindsided by the attack on Pearl Harbor. With hindsight, there was significant evidence that the Japanese

might attempt a direct strike on the naval base, and indeed a number of intelligence briefings shared with Admiral Kimmel, commander of the Pacific Fleet, suggested that the attack was at least a possibility. And yet, as Janis describes it, a kind of fog of groupthink settled over Kimmel and his deputies. The group was convinced that the Japanese would strike somewhere; the question was whether they would declare war by attacking either British or Dutch territories in the Far East. The idea of a direct strike was so far from the consensus view that they made almost no attempt to defend against such an attack, even when they lost radar contact with the Japanese aircraft carriers in the first few days of December. Because the attack was considered low probability, no one bothered to argue for taking the risk seriously. (Janis, 76.)

73 **"Advisers had a way of narrowing"**: Mark Bowden, *The Finish: The Killing of Osama bin Laden* (New York: Grove/Atlantic, Inc., 2012), loc. 159, Kindle.

2: PREDICTING

84 **"One group tended to organize"**: Philip E. Tetlock and Dan Gardner, *Superforecasting: The Art and Science of Prediction* (New York: Crown/ Archetype, 2015), loc. 68–69, Kindle.

85 **"people who are not from Ghana"**: Tetlock and Gardner, loc. 125, Kindle.

86 **"absurd scenes of spaceship pilots"**: Gary Westfahl, Wong Kin Yuen, and Amy Kit-sze Chan, eds., *Science Fiction and the Prediction of the Future: Essays on Foresight and Fallacy* (Jefferson, NC: McFarland, 2011), loc. 82–84, Kindle.

86 **imagine that human beings would colonize Mars**: This same blind spot applies to the people who were actively creating the digital revolution in the 1940s and 1950s. The legendary scientist Vannevar Bush published a much-celebrated essay called "As We May Think" in *The Atlantic* in the late 1940s. It envisioned a new kind of research tool that many consider to be one of the first glimpses of the hypertext universe created by the World Wide Web fifty years later. But Bush's device was not a computer at all; it was a souped-up microfiche machine, where researchers are only able to read static images of documents, and create simple links (Bush calls them "trails") connecting related documents. All the things that make a network-connected computer so powerful— the ability to write your own words, to copy and paste text, to share and

discuss with colleagues—were entirely missing from Bush's vision. And this was coming from the man who had supervised the creation of the very first digital computers ever built.

87 **George Orwell in the 1940s:** Westfahl et al., loc. 195–202, Kindle.

90 **"When his daughter was very ill":** Browne, *Charles Darwin: Voyaging*, 498.

91 **the polluted chaos of London:** The purity of the Malvern water has, in fact, been confirmed using modern scientific methods. The springs flow through unusually hard Precambrian rocks that keep the water largely free of minerals, and the small cracks in the rock function as a kind of natural filter for other impurities.

94 **British ship doctor James Lind:** Druin Burch, *Taking the Medicine: A Short History of Medicine's Beautiful Idea, and Our Difficulty Swallowing It* (London: Vintage, 2010), 158.

94 **He took to maintaining a ledger:** "The first method was the 'dripping sheet,' a wet sheet, slightly wrung out, wrapped around the body and then rubbed vigorously for five minutes. The aim was 'to stimulate the nervous and circulatory systems of the body.' Dr. Gully wrote that 'to very delicate persons I often apply, in the first instance, only friction of the trunk and arms with a wet towel; dry and dress those parts, and then have the legs rubbed in like manner.'" From Keynes, loc. 2888–2896, Kindle.

97 **When a member of Parliament suggested:** "The observations made . . . upon land as well as at sea would be collected, as, if that were done, he anticipated that in a few years, notwithstanding the variable climate of this country, we might know in this metropolis the condition of the weather 24 hours beforehand." From John Gribbin and Mary Gribbin, *FitzRoy: The Remarkable Story of Darwin's Captain and the Invention of the Weather Forecast* (ReAnimus Press, 2016), loc. 4060–4062, Kindle.

97 **Initially the Met Office:** A crude version of this idea had been proposed by Smithsonian secretary Joseph Henry in 1847: "Realising that at least some storms travel from west to east across the North American continent, as early as 1847 Joseph Henry, Secretary of the Smithsonian Institution, proposed a network of telegraphic links to give warnings to citizens of the eastern States of storms coming from the west." From Gribbin, loc. 4151–4153, Kindle.

97 **"Prophecies and predictions they are not":** Peter Moore, "The Birth of the Weather Forecast," www.bbc.com/news/magazine-32483678.

98 **"no notes or calculations"**: Katherine Anderson, *Predicting the Weather: Victorians and the Science of Meteorology* (Chicago: University of Chicago Press, 2010), 119.

98 **They created charts**: "Observers at each of his main stations recorded the temperature, pressure and humidity of the air, the wind speed both at ground level and (from studying cloud movements) at higher altitudes, the state of the sea, how all these parameters had changed since the previous observations, and the amount and kind of precipitation. The information was sent from each observing station at 8 a.m. At ten o'clock in the morning, telegrams are received in Parliament Street, where they are immediately read and reduced, or corrected, for scale-errors, elevation, and temperature; then written into prepared forms, and copied several times. The first copy is passed to the Chief of the department, or his Assistant, with all the telegrams, to be studied for the day's forecasts, which are then carefully written on the first paper, and copied quickly for distribution. At eleven—reports are sent out to the Times (for a second edition), to Lloyd's, and the Shipping Gazette; to the Board of Trade, Admiralty, Horse Guards, and Humane Society. Soon afterward similar reports are sent to other afternoon papers . . ." From Gribbin, loc. 4352–4363.

99 **"Perhaps some day in the dim"**: Lewis Fry Richardson, *Weather Prediction by Numerical Process* (Cambridge, UK: Cambridge University Press, 2007), xi.

105 **"On the real mission"**: Bowden, loc. 195.

108 **"The game determined that Germany"**: Jonathan Keats, "Let's Play War: Could War Games Replace the Real Thing?" http://nautil.us/ issue/28/2050/lets-play-war.

109 **The exercise made it clear**: "Blue, with Saratoga at its center, would sortie from Hawaii and attempt to strike a strategic blow on Black, which was defending the West Coast with Lexington and Langley. As soon as Blue sortied, it was confronted with a screen of five Black submarines, all lying in ambush and tasked with reporting the Blue's movements. Using its aircraft, Blue quickly scouted out and eliminated four of the five submarines, thus providing another early and important lesson on the use of aircraft to counteract submarine forces. It took only a few days for the opposing forces to find one another, yet neither force could gain a clear advantage. In the remaining days of the exercise, one force would attack the other in rolling, far-ranging battles across the seaways of the eastern Pacific, but the territory was too large for one force to dominate. It

proved, however, (a) the viability of carrier airpower to project itself into the combat scenario and (b) the need for more of it." From Phil Keith, *Stay the Rising Sun: The True Story of USS* Lexington, *Her Valiant Crew, and Changing the Course of World War II* (Minneapolis: Zenith Press, 2015), loc. 919–926, Kindle.

110 **"The objective of the game":** http://nautil.us/issue/28/2050/lets -play-war.

114 **"plurality of options":** Paul Hawken, James Ogilvy, and Peter Schwartz, *Seven Tomorrows* (New York: Bantam, 1982), 7.

114 **"[T]he way to solve this":** Pierre Wack, "Scenarios: Uncharted Waters Ahead," *Harvard Business Review*, September 1985.

116 **"A sustained scenario practice":** Pierre Wack, "Living in the Futures," *Harvard Business Review*, May 2013.

117 **Obama later explained:** Bowden, loc. 191, Kindle.

118 **"Our exercise," Klein explains:** Klein, loc. 954–956, Kindle.

120 **Leiter told John Brennan:** Bergen, loc. 191, Kindle.

121 **"McRaven had a backup":** Bergen, loc. 183–184, Kindle.

124 **No one realized it at the time:** Bergen, loc. 171–172, Kindle.

3: MORAL ALGORITHMS

127 **"It must necessarily be understood":** Quoted in Jenny Uglow, *The Lunar Men: Five Friends Whose Curiosity Changed the World* (New York: Farrar, Straus and Giroux, 2002), 169.

128 **"Nature has placed mankind":** Jeremy Bentham, "An Introduction to the Principles of Morals and Legislation," www.econlib.org/library/ Bentham/bnthPML1.html, accessed May 2017.

129 **It is easy to imagine why Bentham:** That utilitarian framework was a cornerstone of George Eliot's philosophical edifice, right next to Ludwig Feuerbach's unconventional theories about love. (She knew the utilitarians well; the *Westminster Review*, where both she and George Henry Lewes published essays and translations, had been originally founded by Bentham himself.) But *Middlemarch* shows just how difficult the emotional calculus of the utilitarians turns out to be in practice.

130 **"1. A description of the potential benefits":** Full text of Executive Order 12291 is available here: www.presidency.ucsb.edu/ws/?pid= 43424.

131 **"Reagan's ideas applied":** Sunstein and Hastie, loc. 1675–1683, Kindle.

132 **an essential justification:** For more information on this, see: https://newrepublic.com/article/81990/obama-cost-benefit-revolution.

133 **"linear value modeling":** "Mathematically, a linear value model represents an alternative's performance score as the weighted sum of its consequences: Overall score = W1X1 + W2X2 + W3X3 + . . . where X1 is the score assigned to measure 1, W1 is the weight or importance assigned to measure 1, X2 is the score assigned to measure 2, W2 is the weight of measure 2, and so on. In order to calculate a meaningful overall score when individual performance measures are recorded in different units (e.g., dollars, hectares, jobs, etc.), the individual performance measure scores must first be 'normalized' and then weighted using some reputable method. Generally, the steps of quantitative value modeling involve: 1 Define the objectives and measures. 2 Identify the alternatives. 3 Assign consequences (or consequence scores) to each alternative on each measure. 4 Assign weights to the measures. 5 Normalize the consequence scores so that they can be aggregated. 6 Calculate the weighted normalized scores (sometimes called 'desirability' scores) to rank alternatives." From Gregory et al, 217.

136 **Google filed patent #8781669:** The full text of the Google patent is available here: www.google.com/patents/US9176500.

4: THE GLOBAL CHOICE

158 **The anti-METI movement:** The argument for the inevitability of our first contact turning out to be with a far more advanced civilization is based on the following assumptions. First, we have been sending structured radio signals from Earth for only the last hundred years. The odds that the first sign of intelligent life would be coming from a society that had only been tinkering with radio for, say, fifty years would be staggeringly long. Think about what would be required for that to happen: on our planet, radio technology takes 13,999,999,880 years to appear, while on some other habitable planet across the galaxy radio just happens to take 13,999,999,930 years to be invented. That would be quite the cosmic coincidence. There may be some recurring progression to the way technological innovation unfolds, but even if there is, it doesn't advance with that level of clockwork. Even a small adjustment in those numbers makes a tremendous difference in terms of technological sophistication. Imagine another planet that deviates from our timetable by just a tenth of 1 percent. If they are more advanced than

us, then they will have been tinkering with radio (and successor technologies) for 14 million years. Of course, depending on where they live in the universe, their radio signals might take millions of years to reach us. But even if you factor in that transmission lag, if we pick up a signal from another galaxy, we will almost certainly find ourselves in conversation with a more advanced civilization.

5: THE PERSONAL CHOICE

191 **"I have delightful plans":** Eliot, loc. 583, Kindle.
192 **"With this good understanding":** Eliot, loc. 7555, Kindle.
195 *Middlemarch* **never lets its reader:** It is true that Eliot was not alone among the Victorian novelists in constructing imaginative forms that embraced multiple scales, from the individual all the way up to the macro movements of history. Dickens's great novels of the 1850s and early 1860s—*Bleak House, Little Dorrit, Our Mutual Friend*—managed to build a vast urban network that connected the lives of street urchins, industrial magnates, withering aristocrats, rentiers and merchants, paper pushers, earnest laborers, and a criminal underworld—all shaped by the new historical forces of industrialization, growing bureaucracy, and metropolitan population explosion. From one angle, Dickens's achievement (similar to Balzac's and to Flaubert's in *Sentimental Education*) is more impressive than Eliot's in *Middlemarch*, given that he had to build a narrative that connected the lives of a city of two million people, as opposed to the small town settings that defined all of Eliot's novels. But in straining to find a form that could make such complicated links of association, Dickens had to sacrifice a certain realism.

The turning points in the Dickensian plot almost never involve a character confronting a complex decision. Their lives change, as their fortunes surge and sag, bounced along by the fairy-tale revelations of secret parentage and hidden wills. But their lives are almost never changed by an individual choice. Where characters must choose between competing options, Dickens almost never pauses to unpack the "frustrating complexity" of the decision, in part because the decisions have all been preordained by his characters' fixed type: the saints take the saintly path; the strivers take the striving path; the villains take the villainous path. Even when the characters have to make a choice, there's nothing to decide. Compare that to Lydgate's vote for the town vicar: the choice is hard precisely because Lydgate's whole personality is in the throes of a slow but discernible transformation from ardent idealist to what we might now call a sellout, compromised by the "threadlike pressures" of a hundred small moral lapses. The drama in the scene—despite the five pages of interior monologue—gets its oxygen from the fact that we honestly don't know what Lydgate will choose in the end, in part because he is a character in the process of changing his skin, but also because the decision is a genuinely hard one.

196 **Lewes was "famously ugly":** Kathryn Hughes, *George Eliot: The Last Victorian* (New York: HarperCollins, 2012), loc. 3386–3393, Kindle.

196 **But over time, a profound bond:** Quoted in Hughes, loc. 134, Kindle.

196 **a journal entry from 1859:** Quoted in Hughes, loc. 143, Kindle.

198 **"I am sure you retain enough":** Cited in Rebecca Mead, *My Life in Middlemarch* (New York: Crown/Archetype, 2014), loc. 77, Kindle.

198 **"My life has deepened unspeakably":** Cited in Mead, loc. 80–81, Kindle.

203 **"[O]rganisms should have":** John Tooby and Leda Cosmides, "Does Beauty Build Adapted Minds? Toward an Evolutionary Theory of Aesthetics, Fiction and the Arts," *SubStance* 30, no. 1/2 (94/95: 2001): 6–27.

209 **As Rebecca Mead writes:** Mead, loc. 223, Kindle.

209 **"a keen vision and feeling":** Eliot, loc. 207, Kindle.

Index